Dave Barry's Complete Guide To Guys

Nicole Peters

DAVE BARRY'S COMPLETE GUIDE TO GUYS
Written by
Jeff Arch
From the book by
Dave Barry
February 2nd, 2004

FADE IN:
EXT. MIAMI - OCEAN AVE, SOUTH BEACH - DAY
Blazing sun. MUSIC everywhere. Everybody's living la vida.

LEOPOLD (V.0.)
And we're good to go.
TWO MEN come out of the BEACON HOTEL. Loud Hawaiian shirts, walking a
Chihuahua. They pause; take in the scene on Ocean.
Adjust their EARPIECES.

LEOPOLD (V.0.)
Proceed to first checkpoint and hold.
They thread their way to the corner... across the street.. .onto the Promenade.
Under fat shady palm trees, to a CLEARING --

CUT TO:
EXT. THE ROOF OF THE BEACON HOTEL - CONTINUOUS
AGENT STEARNS has a RIFLE with a kick-ass scope. AGENT LEOPOLD
watches through binoculars; talks through a collar mike.

LEOPOLD
Okay sit tight. Company's coming.
THROUGH BINOCULARS NOW, as TWO DEADLY MEN approach like
barracudas. A THIRD GUY, BEHIND THEM, the KINGPIN they're protecting.
Then as TREETOPS BLOCK THE VIEW --

LEOPOLD
Shit. Hang on.
Leopold scans, looking for them. Searching, until he FINDS --

LEOPOLD
WHOA --

The Hawaiian Shirt Guys hear that. The SEE the Barracudas, getting nearer; steal a look at the roof...

CUT TO:
POV FROM ROOFTOP - THROUGH BINOCULARS - A FANTASTIC BLONDE rinses off at an outdoor shower. Beads of spray skip off her like diamonds in the sunlight.

2.
STEARNS
Oh, mama.
She bends, twists; water streams down every delicious curve.

LEOPOLD
She sure is taking her time...

STEARNS
She must be really salty...

LEOPOLD
(shakes his head)
It's not just the salt. She's got sunscreen on. Then the sand gets on that, and it sticks...
(then still watching)
Hell, one time I was in Hawaii? And these three models --

STEARNS
Wait a minute.
(looks at him)
Hawaii.

LEOPOLD
-- Shit!
He WHIPS THE BINOCULARS back: but all that's left is the Chihuahua. Then, walking into the spot --

DAVE
Hi, I'm Dave Barry. Has something like this ever happened to you?
(bends down to pet

THE CHIHUAHUA)

Because if you're a guy - or if you know someone who is - then what you've just seen should look pretty familiar.

He picks up the Chihuahua, starts walking with it.

DAVE

Scientists call this condition "Lust Induced Brain Freeze." It affects millions of guys, every day, in all walks of life -- causing anything from a mild embarrassment, to an international incident.

He stops. Finds LEOPOLD and STEARNS and SEVERAL OTHER AGENTS pointing GUNS at him.

3.

LEOPOLD

Hand over the dog.

DAVE

Hey. I didn't even know it was a dog.

They take it from him; rush it away. Dave turns to CAMERA.

DAVE

Notice I didn't say it's a condition that affects men every day -- only guys. And that subtle but important difference is one of the things this movie is about.

CUT TO:

INT. LIVING ROOM - NIGHT

A HUSBAND and his WIFE. He has suitcases by the front door.

WIFE

You'll never get away with this.
I'll sue you down to your last penny.

HUSBAND

Good luck - I transferred everything we own into private accounts, where you can't touch it. In fact, as of now, you're broke.

WIFE

But...why?

HUSBAND

I've fallen in love with another woman. A younger woman. Prettier, with no cellulite. Actually, I think you'd like her.

WIFE
You bastard.
The IMAGE FREEZES. Dave walks into the room.

DAVE
Now clearly, this woman is dealing with a Man.
(MORE)

4.
DAVE (CONT'D)
Whereas Guys aren't capable of doing anything like what you just saw. Guys are more like this:

CUT TO:
INT. A BAR/RESTAURANT - NIGHT
A DIFFERENT HUSBAND sits across from his WIFE. Above and behind her is a TV with SportsCenter on.

WIFE
I just want you to know, I've thought about this a lot.

GUY HUSBAND
Mm.

WIFE
And I've talked it over with everyone I know.

GUY HUSBAND
(NODS)
Good.
She looks down; stirs her soda.

WIFE
So there's nothing left to do now, but leave you, forever, and only see you from across a shiny conference table with bloodthirsty lawyers all around it.

GUY HUSBAND

(a beat; turns to her)
-- Okay.

WIFE
"Okay?" That's all you have to say?
(then watching him)
Well then I guess this is it.
She pushes back from the table, starts off.

GUY HUSBAND
Wait a minute.

(THEN)
This can't be happening...
The words she's waited for. She turns, relieved.

GUY HUSBAND
(to the tv)
How can you dQ that? How can you trade Lupenza?
(then to the BARTENDER)
What's the matter with these people?

BARTENDER
Beats me. I saw this on the eight o'clock.

GUY HUSBAND
He's the backbone of the whole team!
They're pikers without Lupenza!

WIFE
I'll see you in court.

GUY HUSBAND
-- I gotta call Lenny.
He takes out his cell phone. She levels a look.

WIFE
Maybe you should call your lawyer too.

GUY HUSBAND

5

If he could hit left-handed pitching,
I would.

(THEN)
Lenny. Pick up -- the Yankees got Lupenza!
The IMAGE FREEZES.

CUT TO:
EXT. A FRONT PORCH - DAY
Two OLD PEOPLE on a glider. LENORE talks directly to CAMERA.
ALBERT'S absorbed with some device that we can't see.

LENORE
Well when I met him, I didn't know so much. About guys, or men or what have
you -- we just didn't talk about such things then. In fact, I didn't see him naked
until quite well into our marriage. When was it Albert?

6.
ALBERT
A year ago. By accident.

LENORE
Anyway. I thought I was marrying a man, but didn't know that in his heart, he was
a guy.

DAVE (O.S.)
When did you first suspect?

LENORE
Not long after the wedding. But it didn't bother me. I just didn't know how to
recognize the signs.
But we've learned to live with it.
Haven't we, Albert?
(then after a beat)
Albert.

ALBERT
It's twelve hundred and thirty-one miles from this spot right here, to Cleveland.

LENORE

What does that have to do with anything?
He holds up the device - handheld GPS.

ALBERT
Six hundred fifty-one from Atlanta.

LENORE
Who cares how far we are from Atlanta?

ALBERT
You have a cousin there.

LENORE
Albert. There's a person here asking us questions. There's a film crew here.
He looks up at the CAMERA, as if just noticing someone there.
Then holding up the GPS --

ALBERT
You. Where do you live.

DAVE (O.S.)
Here in Miami.

ALBERT
What part.
Lenore buries her head.

CUT TO:
EXT. MIAMI BEACH - DAY
Dave walks down a crowded street. Colorful day life.

DAVE
Like a lot of big cities, Miami is known for its sizeable population of guys. So we came here to take the city's pulse on the subject.

CUT TO:
INT. A SECRETARY'S OFFICE CUBICLE - DAY
A young, pretty, single SECRETARY.

SECRETARY

Let me put it this way. Everyone I ever dated was a male. I mean they were all men. But only some of them were guys. You know?

DAVE (O.S.)
I see.

SECRETARY
(thinks about it)
-- The guys were funnier. But the men were more responsible. You could almost half-believe them when they told you something sometimes.

DAVE (O.S.)
So, if you were to meet someone that was funny and responsible...

SECRETARY
That would be a woman.

CUT TO:
EXT. EQUESTRIAN ESTATE - STABLES - DAY
A 20-ish HORSE GROOMER talks to the CAMERA while she combs out a mane.

8.
HORSE GROOMER
Well guys, they're sort of like your older brother. And men are like your dad.

DAVE (O.S.)
In what way?

HORSE GROOMER
Your older brother doesn't have to grow up. Your dad came that way.

CUT TO:
EXT. BARN - DAY
Dave walks out of the barn towards CAMERA.

DAVE
So now you have some background on basic guy attributes. But before we move on, let's look at one more scene and see where you stand --

CUT TO:

TITLE CARD: "ROGER AND ELAINE"
INT. ELAINE'S LIVING ROOM - DAY
ELAINE works at a window desk. ROGER watches NFL on FOX.

JOHN MADDEN
(ON TV)
-- now that's the kind of middle linebacker you like to see. He's got the mud all over him, he's got the bleeding knuckles, he's got the clumps of grass all jammed in his

HELMET --
ELAINE
Roger?

ROGER
(to the tv)
Oh man you gotta show that again Shepauses; chews her pen...

ELAINE
Roger...I think I really love you.
(MORE)

9
ELAINE (CONT'D)
(looks over there)
But I can't bear the uncertainty anymore, of where this relationship is going.
Roger turns...

ELAINE
I'm not asking whether you want to get married. Only whether you believe that we have some kind of a future together. That you, and I - have a future.

JOHN MADDEN
Now this is just what you want in a playoff game. You got snow, you got mud, you got a lead that keeps changing, you got two great teams that just hate each other to the bone and would rather die than give up...
Roger looks...then takes the REMOTE and TURNS OFF THE TV - waving Elaine over, who cuddles into him.

ROGER

I've been thinking too, Elaine. And for the first time in my life, I'm feeling like I might really be close to a lasting commitment. I haven't said anything up until now because it's always been important to me that I not mislead you. But yes, Elaine. I want to think that we dQ have a future. And with a little more time, I think I could be sure.

ELAINE
Oh, Roger...
He smiles. Strokes her hair and pulls her in even closer.
They share a long deep sigh together, As the PICTURE FREEZES and DAVE WALKS IN.

DAVE
If this was how you responded, you're not a guy. You may not even exist.
(then taking the remote)
On the other hand...

10.
ROGER AND ELAINE DIGITALLY REWIND BACK TO THEIR EARLIER POSITIONS. DAVE RESTARTS THE ACTION AS ELAINE IS SAYING --
ELAINE
I'm not asking whether you want to get married. Only whether you believe that we have some kind of a future together. That you, and I - have a future.
(then looking at him)
Roger?

ROGER
(engrossed in game)
What.
FREEZE on her look, and --

DAVE
(TO CAMERA)
If that was you...you're a guy.

CUT TO:
INT. A DRESSING ROOM - NIGHT
SHERYL CROW talks to the CAMERA before going onstage. The muffled SOUNDS of the warmup band O.S.

SHERYL CROW

Well there were always guys at my shows - right from the beginning. I mean you start out playing beer halls, right? So when you have beer, you have guys. And it sorta just grew from there. But I was okay with it.
They didn't cause much trouble.

DAVE (O.S.)

And what about men.

SHERYL CROW

Men cause trouble.

(THEN)

But that's okay too. I get half my songs from that.

DAVE (O.S.)

So it all works out.

11.
SHERYL CROW

Long as they buy the records...

CUT TO:
INT. MIAMI PUBLIC LIBRARY - DAY

Dave walks along the stacks in the ANTHROPOLOGY SECTION.

DAVE

So where did this all start? Many experts now think they know where men came from, but what about Guys? where did they come from?
He stops, peels off a THICK BOOK full of science things.

DAVE

To answer this question accurately, we might have to look something up.
So instead we'll travel back to prehistoric sub-Saharan Africa, and get there just in time for the Dawn of Guys.

CUT TO:
TITLE CARD: "THE DAWN OF GUYS"
CUT TO:

EXT. PREHISTORIC AFRICA - MOONLIGHT

The endless expanse. A cluster of caves. SOUND EFX of all kinds of nasty shit out there. Skittering over rocks.

Slithering through the grasses. Bigger predators, circling...

A ROOSTER cocks his head back and CROWS out.

CUT TO:

TNT. ONE OF THE CAVES

PRIMATE ROGER opens one eye...SEES PRIMATE ELAINE, PRIMATE KIDS and PRIMATE IN-LAWS. Hairy grunting things, all sleeping in a protective clump...

12.

He rolls over, back to sleep. But the ROOSTER CROWS again...

CUT TO:

THE ROOSTER, COOKING ON AN OPEN FIRE

CUT TO:

EXT. THE CAVES - MORNING

PRIMATE ROGER comes out. A sleepy nod at PRIMATE GENE and OTHER PRIMATES, as they take up LARGE JAGGED ROCK SLABS leaning against their caves and start off. In a few million years they'll be leaving suburban driveways this way.

EXT. TRAIL FROM CAVE AREA - CAVES IN B.G. - MORNING

PRIMATE ROGER and PRIMATE GENE have joined PRIMATE LENNY and PRIMATE PHIL. All carrying their slabs of jagged rocks.

PRIMATE ROGER

Grunt grunt grunt grunt grunt!

(SUBTITLE)

0

-- and that's why wildebeests are so mean.

PRIMATE GENE

Grunt grunt!0
Ha ha!

PRIMATE LENNY

Grunt grunt grunt! 0
That's really funny!

PRIMATE PHIL
Grunt ...0
I don't get it...
The other three look at him.

EXT. THE CAVE AREA - DAY
PRIMATE WOMEN work in stooped-over positions, trying to pound roots and tend fires while BABY PRIMATES crawl all over them.
They HEAR the Primate Guys' laughter trailing off. They trade looks; Something seems to pass between them...

EXT. HUNTING GROUNDS - DAY
Primates Roger, Gene, Lenny and Phil get to the grounds and SEE PRIMATES PETE and LOUIE already there. These two don't have the rock slabs though.

13
PRIMATE ROGER
Grunt grunt?0
Whassup?

PRIMATE PETE
Grunt grunt grunt. 0
Nothing. We've been hunting.

PRIMATE GENE
Grunt grunt? 0
Where are your jagged rock slabs?

PRIMATE LOUIE
Grunt? ❏
Slabs?
(looks at Primate

PETE)
Grunt grunt grunt? ❏
Who needs slabs?

Primate Pete laughs with him; then holds up a ROUND ROCK, about the size of a grapefruit. Primate Roger and Primate Gene trade looks with Primate Lenny and Primate Phil.

Grunting/subtitles continue.

FIRST FOUR PRIMATES
Ooooohhhh.
Ooooohhhh.

PRIMATE ROGER
Where'd you get that?

PRIMATE PETE
Primate Discount Manny. He just got them in.

PRIMATE ROGER
Mind if I have a look?

PRIMATE PETE
Be my guest.
He hands it over. Primate Roger lays down his jagged rock slab to check it out. His buddies gather round.

PRIMATE GENE
How do you kill an animal with that?

PRIMATE LOUIE
You throw it.

14.
PRIMATE LENNY
You mean you don't chase the old ones until they get tired and then hit them with the jagged rock slabs?

PRIMATE PETE
(shakes his head)
You can stand in one place all day.
And when they go by, you just let loose.
He shows a throwing motion. The first four look intrigued.

PRIMATE LOUIE
You can carry more than one - and if you're throwing uphill, it rolls back down if you miss. It's so much easier with these.

PRIMATE GENE
-- I'm sticking with mine.
(then off their looks)
We've been using these jagged slabs forever. And you know why? Because they work. And anyway, killing them is only half of it -- how are you gonna skin a wildebeest with that?
They look at Primate Pete: Yeah, how? But he's there.

PRIMATE PETE
We get the women to do it.
They look among themselves. They like it. But then.

PRIMATE ROGER
How?

PRIMATE PETE
-- I'm working on it.

CUT TO:
EXT. THE CAVE AREA - SUNSET
The PRIMATE WOMEN are still, pounding roots and tending fires and dealing with climbing PRIMATE KIDS. They HEAR SHOUTS O.S.; gather and go to the ridge where they SEE

POV FROM RIDGE --
The PRIMATE GUYS are coming back, without their jagged slabs and without any animals. But they are having great fun:

15. running in primitive patterns, and throwing one of the ROCKS back and forth and chasing whoever has it. It looks like the beginnings of rugby, or Australian Rules Football, in terms of all they need now is beer.
The PRIMATE WOMEN watch. And trade looks. Once more, something seems to pass between them...

CUT TO:
INT. PRIMATE CAVE - NIGHT

Primate Roger and Primate Elaine try to keep it down for the Primate Kids' sake.

PRIMATE ELAINE
(grunting, subtitled)
Please don't tell me you got rid of your jagged rock slab.

PRIMATE ROGER
But these are great!

PRIMATE ELAINE
But you didn't kill anything.

PRIMATE ROGER
Nobody's going with jagged slabs anymore.

PRIMATE ELAINE
But the kids are hungry.

PRIMATE ROGER
What about your pounded roots?

PRIMATE ELAINE
Pounded roots are a side dish. They need balance in their diets.
(then off his look)
And another thing - suppose you do start bringing animals home using this -- who's going to skin and clean them?
He looks at her-the SOUND of TOMORROW'S ROOSTER CROWING as

CUT TO:
EXT. THE CAVE - MORNING
Primate Roger comes out of the cave, with his rock. He gives it such a look.

16.
Then looking up at the sky he hurls it, up as high as he can...

AND THE CAMERA FOLLOWS THE ROCK, UP, UP, IN SLOW MOTION, PEAKING, THEN STARTING ITS DESCENT BACK TO EARTH -- ONLY NOW
IT'S NOT A ROCK BUT A WINDOWS --
CUT TO:

INT. ROGER AND ELAINE'S LIVING ROOM - NIGHT
-- which ROGER is holding, across from ELAINE on the couch.

ELAINE
Five hundred dollars?

ROGER
It can hold a thousand addresses.

ELAINE
So can my address book.

ROGER
Can your address book pick up your em-ail?

ELAINE
No but my computer can.

ROGER
Well this can do both.

ELAINE
For five hundred dollars it should give me a manicure, Roger! It should drive me home from work at night!
HOW could you spend that kind of money without discussing it first?
On Roger's look...the PICTURE FREEZES. Dave walks in.

DAVE
There's a whole list of things a guy is supposed to discuss first.
Unfortunately, he never knows what they are until he's already not discussed them.
(MORE)

17.
DAVE (CONT'D)
To a girl it's a pain in the butt.
But to a guy - some things just come naturally...

CUT TO:
EXT. THE PROW OF A SHIP - DAY

Shrouded in fog. EXPLORER ROGER scans the horizon through a spyglass. Next to him is long-suffering EXPLORER ELAINE.

EXPLORER ELAINE
Well did you ask?

EXPLORER ROGER
This is a shortcut.
Explorer Elaine shakes her head. Dave enters.

DAVE
There's a very simple reason why guys don't ask for directions. It's because they know that if they do, someone else - most likely Visigoths - will come and steal their woman.
CAMERA PANS to the side rails, where a CLUSTER OF HUNGRY VISIGOTHS nod, slobbering, confirming this.

EXPLORER ELAINE
I just want to get to Colonial America.

CUT TO:
TITLE CARD: "GUYS IN COLONIAL AMERICA"
EXT. BOSTON HARBOR - NIGHT
A bunch of GUYS dressed as Indians are throwing barrels into the water. A COLONIAL REPORTER interviews COLONIAL ROGER.

COLONIAL REPORTER
-- and this is your way of expressing the public outrage over the high- handed anti-democratic actions of the British Government in general and King George III in specific?

COLONIAL ROGER
(looks a little nervous)
Uh, yeah.

18.
COLONIAL REPORTER
Might I ask, sir, whose idea was this?

COLONIAL ROGER

(POINTS)
Guy over there.

COLONIAL REPORTER
The one drinking coffee?

COLONIAL ROGER
That's him. His name's Starbuck.
He said to get rid of all the tea.

COLONIAL REPORTER
(NODS; THEN)
I see. One more question. Aren't those Greek fraternity letters painted on your chest?
The Guy looks; GREEK LETTERS in greasepaint.

COLONIAL ROGER
I didn't do that.
(then as the Reporter

WAITS)
Don't tell anyone.

CUT TO:
EXT. MIAMI - OUTDOOR CAFE - DAY
FOUR MIAMI GIRLS, ethnically cross-sectioned. LILA. MIA.

SIDRA. KARLA E.
LILA
Well that's pretty much how it is right now, right? They don't grow up. Or, they grow up, but they don't change.

MIA
(NODS)
You want to know how to spot a guy, there's your first clue: Look for an otherwise man who did not grow up.

SIDRA
No they grow up all right -- but only just enough - you know?
(MORE)

19.
SIDRA (CONT'D)
Like they'll meet the absolute minimum requirements of being a man, but that's it.
The rest of the time they're fourth-graders. Walking fourth-graders.

KARLA E
More like driving fourth graders.

SIDRA
With credit cards.

LILA
And a phone.

MIA
And give them ten minutes on their own? Or put them in with other guys?
Now you've gone nuclear.

KARLA E
Please.

CUT TO:
EXT. BURGER KING - DAY
The lot is filled with 60's and 70's cars. Dave gets out of a CHEVY VEGA; has
mutton-chop sideburns, talks to CAMERA.

DAVE
In learning to understand Guys today, it's important to remember that these same
guys, only yesterday, were just kids.

CUT TO :
INT. BURGER KING - DAY
A table of 8 YEAR OLD BOYS: punching, eating, climbing all over each other.
One poor luckless DAD with them.

BURGER KING DAD
Stop punching!

BURGER KING KID

We're not punching!

BURGER KING DAD
You are too punching - now stop! We didn't come here to punch!

20.
They stop; look at him as if he's crazy. Then one of them notices ROGER AT 8 looking O.S.

BURGER KING KID
Hey Roger's got a girlfriend.

ROGER AT 8
I do not!

BURGER KING KID
Then what're you looking at!

ROGER AT 8
Nothing!
And they start punching again. The Dad looks up - so weary...

DAVE
(AT COUNTER)
Here we can see where even at an early age, guy behavior is already well developed along complex patterns that social scientists have called,
"jerks." While girls at the same age are referred to by the same social scientists, as "human beings."

ANGLE ON A TABLE FULL OF GIRLS - INCLUDING ELAINE AT AGE 8
They are all chatting nicely, passing out napkins and ketchup packets making sure everyone has what they need. While the MOTHER that brought them quietly reads a novel.

DAVE
See? Humans.
He walks past with his takeout order. As ELAINE at 8 notices Roger, blushing, taking all this punishment because of her.

BURGER KING DAD

(as Dave exits)
Will you please stop punching!

CUT TO:
INT. NOTED PEDIATRICIAN'S OFFICE - DAY
Dave sits across from a BRITISH GUY with a SUBTITLE saying,
"Noted Pediatrician. " He has a laser pointer and a powerpoint presentation.

21.
DAVE
Where are we in the area of Guy Violence, Doctor.

SCIENTIFIC EXPERT
Well first, one must understand the inherent differences in DNA and cell structure
as relates to men and women.

(CLICKING SLIDES)
For example, all women have a gene that makes them have the need for
meaningful conversations. Likewise, all men have a gene in them that we scientists
believe is directly related to violence.

DAVE
And what can be done about that.

SCIENTIFIC EXPERT well, some of my esteemed colleagues are quite keen on
the idea of tampering with the DNA itself - an idea with which I heartily disagree.
The bastards...

DAVE
Then what would you recommend.

SCIENTIFIC EXPERT
Me? Well they can start by spreading out the funding a little bit. Let a few other
scientists wet their beaks.
I mean what's the point of rewarding the same tired old hacks, year after

YEAR --
DAVE
I meant about Guy Violence.

SCIENTIFIC EXPERT
OH --
(then shifting back)
Well nothing, really. I mean, what can you do. Short of lobotomizing them, anyway. No I suppose we'll just have to continue to channel their aggression into socially acceptable outlets. Like professional wrestling, or the space program.

DAVE
I see. Can I ask you a question?

22.
SCIENTIFIC EXPERT
Certainly.

DAVE
Where'd you get that laser pointer.

SCIENTIFIC EXPERT
It's mine.

CUT TO:
EXT. TOY WORLD WAREHOUSE PLANET - DAY
Dave stands in front of the entrance.

DAVE
A lot of work has been done in the field of children's toys and how they unconsciously reinforce gender roles. Studies have found that over ninety-three per cent of this work is done by researchers who don't have children of their own. But to test the theory anyway, we're here at Toy World Warehouse Planet.

CUT TO:
INT. TOY WORLD WAREHOUSE PLANET - DAY
Dave shepherds new father GENE up to the CUSTOMER HELP counter.

DAVE
Hi! My friend here is looking for toys for his son that are gender neutral, environmentally sound, and culturally unbiased!

SALES GUY
Here it is.

He brings up a box with a picture of a spinning top on it.

NEW FATHER GENE
What's it do?

SALES GUY
It's recyclable.

23.
NEW FATHER GENE
Where are the trucks and guns.

CUT TO:
EXT. TOY WORLD PARKING LOT - DAY
New Father Gene meets up with NEW MOTHER KELLY at the car.
She came from GROCERY WORLD; he helps load up the bags...

NEW MOTHER KELLY
What's this?

NEW FATHER GENE
(looks, sees the toy

STORE BOX)
Oh I got that for Benjy.

NEW MOTHER KELLY
You were supposed to get a rattle.

NEW FATHER GENE
All the rattles were recalled.

NEW MOTHER KELLY
So you bought a tank.

NEW FATHER GENE
Wait'll you see what this can do, baby. Benjy's gonna love it.

NEW MOTHER KELLY
Oh yeah? Can he shake it? Will it rattle?

NEW FATHER GENE

Rattle? This thing'll bring down a bookshelf!

She looks at him. He'll be returning the thing within seconds. CAMERA PANS to Dave, who shrugs.

CUT TO:

EXT. DETROIT - ED'S AUTO SHOP - DAY

A rundown place with junked cars out front. ED's an intense little guy in a Tigers' hat and a couple major tattoos.

ED

Well I'm into fireworks. I like to take 'em apart, you know. And study 'em. See what makes 'em tick.

24.

He shows Dave a box with ASSORTED FIREWORKS inside.

ED

I just got these from Ohio. I don't think they're as good as the ones I got from Tennessee. Not as loud, you know?

DAVE

Well no, if loud is your --

ED

If you want to hear loud - listen to this.

He goes over to a different box, takes out what looks like a stick of dynamite. Gets ready to light it; turns to CAMERA.

ED

You may want to step back a couple hundred yards.

CUT TO:

INT. DAVE'S CAR - TRAVELING - DAY

As Ed's Auto Shop recedes in the background - with a LOUD EXPLOSION accompanying -

DAVE

So when we see guys like Ed, and his fireworks - or guys shooting marine flares into innocent pumpkins, or building catapults that'll throw a Buick - we should not condemn them.

We should not assume these are just pointless juvenile activities.

Instead we should be convinced they are, and move on to Guys in the Workplace.

CUT TO:
EXT. CITY STREET - PHILADELPHIA - DAY
A PHILADELPHIA GIRL stands outside a CHEESESTEAK PLACE.

PHILADELPHIA GIRL
Guys at work? Or guys doing work.
(MORE)

25.
PHILADELPHIA GIRL (CONT'D)
I mean unless you want to talk about faxing or emailing their stupid jokes back and forth. Sick jokes.

CUT TO:
EXT. WALL STREET - DAY
Dave and a SEASONED BROKER eat HOT DOGS from a CORNER CART.

BROKER
Ten, fifteen years ago? A guy would call you up with some joke he just heard. So you wanna pass it on, it's by phone. One person at a time.
Then a while later, some guy calls you up with the same exact joke.
Then when group faxing came in, it really sped things up. Next thing you know there's like ten faxes on your machine, from places you never even heard of. Places around the world, I'm saying.

DAVE
And how long would that take.

BROKER
A run of the mill, 'guy walks into a bar' joke, those'd take about .a. week to come back to you. The topical ones, your mass murders and tragic accidents and the like, they're naturally gonna have a lot more heat on them and they'll circulate a lot quicker. I mean no one's gonna sit on a Princess Diana joke until three weeks after the crash. No one i know, anyway.

26

(THEN CHEWING)
Now there's the internet -- and what used to take a week'll take like seconds. I'm telling you it's getting harder and harder to keep up.

DAVE
A lot of people don't understand the attention and the kind of importance these jokes have.

BROKER
Who.
(MORE)

26.
BROKER (CONT'D)
(THEN)
Oh you mean women? Well, you know - what's the importance of having fifteen pairs of shoes?

DAVE
No one knows that.

CUT TO:
TITLE CARD: "ROGER AND ELAINE"
INT. ELAINE'S CAR - DAY
Roger is slumped across the back seat; messed-up clothes and in obvious pain. Elaine drives; talks to CAMERA.

ELAINE
So I get this call at work.
(then to Roger back

THERE)
You want to tell this?

ROGER
Its just a sprain.

ELAINE
(shakes her head)

I get on the phone and they say he's okay - but maybe I should come down to the paper and get him. Does he look okay?

ROGER
It's a sprain. It just looks worse.

ELAINE
Not the way I heard it.

CUT TO:
TNT. NEWSPAPER BUILDING - EARLIER THAT DAY
Roger's at his desk; can't help but HEAR PATRICK, TOM and GENE talking nearby.

PATRICK
He's how old?

TOM
High school. A sophomore.

27.
GENE
Big deal. I could run the forty that fast.

TOM
You and who - the Flash? This kid set a national record.

GENE
Yeah? What nation.

BACK TO:
TNT. ELAINE'S CAR - CONTINUING
ELAINE
(TO ROGER)
Tell me something. If the article was about a poem there wouldn't be an argument - would there.

ROGER
Why would there be an article about a poem.

ELAINE
I'm just saying. I don't see the four of you fighting over who can write the better sonnet.

ROGER
So?

ELAINE
So no one gets hurt writing sonnets.

ROGER
(off her look; then)
It's a sprain.

BACK TO:
INT. THE NEWSPAPER BUILDING - DAY
Roger listens more agitated as the argument mounts.

GENE
When did you last run the forty?

PATRICK
Hey. I could beat you in the forty running backwards.

28.
TOM
You couldn't even beat your butt running backwards.

ROGER
(from his desk)
Will you guys cut it out?
They stop. Look at him.

ROGER
The kid in the story's in high school.
You're not. You're supposed to be adults and you're bragging about who can beat who in a stupid footrace.

TOM
No one's bragging.

PATRICK
Gene's just saying he can run the forty in under six seconds.

ROGER
Hey. I can do it in under six seconds.
FREEZE THE PICTURE, on their expressions. BRING UP "CHARIOTS

OF FIRE" MUSIC
DISSOLVE T0:
EXT. CITY PARK - DAY
The FOUR GUYS crouch in their starting stance. A SECRETARY stands at the end of a marked-off course with a stopwatch and a whistle. She blows the whistle. They're off.

SLOW MOTION WITH MUSIC
All four guys explode off the line. Patrick gets five strides and goes down. Tom gets two more and falls, howling in pain.
Then Gene and Roger, neck and neck for at least three more strides until Roger HEARS A "POP," that ECHOES over the music, and goes toppling down. As Gene finishes alone - gripping his side in awful pain but pumping his fist in victory.

29.
MUSIC FADES AS
DISSOLVE TO:
INT. ELAINE'S APARTMENT - NIGHT
Elaine comes in; Roger, limping and leaning heavily on her.

ELAINE
I don't know why I listened to you.
You need to see a doctor.

ROGER
It's a sprain, Elaine.

ELAINE
Roger you can't walk.

ROGER

It'll work itself out.
She gives him a look. Parks him long enough to close the door behind him. Without her support, he drops to the floor.
She turns to the CAMERA.

ELAINE
Why won't they go to the doctor?

CUT TO:
INT. DOCTOR'S OFFICE - DAY
British, white coat, stethoscope.

DOCTOR
Here's why.
He holds up a RUBBER GLOVE. Dangles it harmlessly.

DOCTOR
I don't care who they are. If they think there's even a chance their doctor will use one of these - and they always assume there is - they won't come in.
(MORE)

30.
DOCTOR (CONT'D)
(puts it away, shakes

HIS HEAD)
If there's anything out there that would bring them in... it hasn't been invented yet.

CUT TO:
TITLE CARD: "THE FANTASY GUY MEDICAL CLINIC"
EXT. FANTASY GUY MEDICAL CLINIC - DAY
It says so on the SIGN. ANOTHER SIGN, like an international road sign, has a graphic of a HAND IN A RUBBER GLOVE with a RED LINE through it. There are also SPORTS TEAM BANNERS.

CUT TO:
INT. EXAM ROOM - DAY
The DOCTOR checks a GUY'S chart. There's a TV with ESPN on in the exam room.

GUY DOCTOR
What seems to be the problem?

GUY PATIENT
Well the main thing is, I keep coughing up blood. And I get these really severe chest pains, and double vision sometimes. And every night at sunset, little worms come burrowing out of my skin.

GUY DOCTOR
It's just a sprain.

GUY PATIENT
That's what I thought.

CUT TO:
TITLE CARD: "GUY FEELINGS"
INT. MIAMI - OUTDOOR CAFE - DAY
Karla E, Mia, Lila and Sidra again, with Dave.

DAVE
A lot has been said about how guys don't share their feelings.

31
KARLA E
You mean they have them?

MIA
Or they have them and don't acknowledge them.

LILA
Or they don't think that others have them.

SIDRA
Or they just don't think.

DAVE
(as they agree on

THAT)

-- Is it possible that they do have feelings, they do acknowledge them and they do know others have them - but they just don't express it the same way?

Four blank faces look at him. Then.

KARLA E
Sports. They have feelings about sports.

LILA
And their underwear.

(POLLS THEM)
You ever try and throw out their underwear?

MIA
Once. I nearly lost my life.

SIDRA
They act like it's so sacred. I've seen pairs of briefs with holes in them larger than the leg holes.
(as the others nod)
I tried to throw a pair out once?
And sneak it past him? He went out into the garbage and found them. He said he couldn't trust me after that.

KARLA E
Tell me what that's all about.

SIDRA
I don't even want to think about it.

32.
DAVE
(off their reactions)
So you agree then, that guys at least have feelings.

MIA
They just waste them. That's all.

CUT TO:
EXT. SUBURBAN TOWNHOUSE - NIGHT

ROGER and ELAINE get out of Roger's car. Elaine has an armload of magazines.

ELAINE
Now remember. Gene's dad is real sick. Kelly says he doesn't talk about it. So see if you can draw him out.

ROGER
He already did talk about it.

ELAINE
Oh? What did he say?

ROGER
He said his dad is real sick.
She gives him a look. Gets to the door.

ROGER
What are those?

ELAINE
Kelly's boss is turning forty.

ROGER
So you're giving her magazines?

ELAINE
(a look; then)
Just see if you can get him to talk.

CUT TO:
INT. DEN - NIGHT
There's a GAME on. Gene sort of stares. Roger has a SHOEBOX on his lap; goes through Gene's SEGA cartridges.

33.
ROGER
Galaxians. Far out...

GENE
(while Roger keeps

LOOKING)
Can you believe the Yankees got Lupenza.

ROGER
They get everybody.

GENE
I know. They suck.

ROGER
I know.
Silence. Roger pulls out two cartridges, compares them.

GENE
I got to Level 24 of Arkanoids.

ROGER
(TURNS)
-- You're kidding.
Gene shakes his head. He's not. This is big.

ROGER
You've seen the Evil Presence?
(then off his look)
What's it look like?
Gene shrugs; even the best of friends. Roger understands.
CAMERA PANS to Dave.

DAVE
Believe it or not, ladies - that was sharing.
(then nods to kitchen)
And believe it or not, guys - so is

THIS --
CUT TO:
INT. KITCHEN - NIGHT
Elaine and Kelly with magazines and writing pads.

ELAINE

Well I don't know. How do you think she feels about getting older?

34
KELLY
I don't know... I know how I felt.
How did you feel about it?

ELAINE
How does anybody feel.

KELLY
(NODS)
So you think she'll want a smaller gathering?

ELAINE
Well if we go that way, we know who to invite.

KELLY
But then who do we not invite.

ELAINE
Exactly. And how are they going to feel about that.

KELLY
So maybe we should make it a slightly larger gathering.

ELAINE
-- Depends on the food, I guess. I mean, if we go with a larger gathering...

KELLY
Exactly.

ELAINE
(finds the right

MAGAZINE)
I saw something earlier in here about low-fat hors d'oeuvres.

KELLY
Oh - I've seen that one too.

They open to the article, scanning it.

ELAINE
Hmm.

KELLY
Hmm.

35.
ELAINE
You thinking what I'm thinking?

KELLY
That if we have low fat hors d'oeuvres she'll think we noticed she's gaining weight?

ELAINE
Exactly.

KELLY
(CONSIDERS THAT)
Maybe just blow it out, you know? I mean it's a party. Go with the high fat.

ELAINE
Thinking she won't think we've noticed the weight gain.

KELLY
Unless she thinks that's insensitive.
You know, that we hadn't noticed...

ELAINE
Hmm...
They close the magazine, look through the others when:

KELLY
How about medium fat hors d'oeuvres?

ELAINE
And we could cut them into smaller pieces?

KELLY

(THEN)
She could think we were being cheap.

ELAINE
And how would she feel about that...

CUT TO:
INT. THE DEN - SAME
Roger and Gene watch a PORSCHE COMMERCIAL without the sound.

GENE
That one has the GPS. With the screen that has maps of everything?

36.
ROGER
What about with the convertible.

GENE
It's optional on the convertible.
Unless you get the turbo, then it's standard.

ROGER
Phil Wonkerman got the turbo.

GENE
No shit...Phil got a Porsche?

ROGER
Said it was his birthday present to himself.

GENE
(IMPRESSED; THEN)
When was his birthday.

ROGER
Beats me. Probably around the same time when he got the car.

GENE
No shit...

(THEN)
Maybe we should get him something.

ROGER
(looks at him)
He just got a Porsche.

GENE
Right.
They look at the TV again. Then, from the kitchen doorway:

ELAINE
Roger?
They turn. Elaine gives Roger a look. PICTURE FREEZES AS:

37.
DAVE
Roger met Elaine at a company event.

CUT TO:
EXT. A HOTEL POOL - DAY
PEOPLE with NAMETAGS mingle with drinks and appetizers.
Dave comes away from the hot buffet table with a great haul.

DAVE
-- They discovered they had something in common right away.
He points to ROGER and ELAINE, over by a tiki-torch.

ELAINE
You're kidding! That was you? At the Burger King?

ROGER
I was in fourth grade.

ELAINE
I was too! But my God, you remembered that?

DAVE
(off Roger's nod)
She loved that he remembered that.

CUT TO:
INT. A BOWLING ALLEY - NIGHT
A GLOW-BOWL night; neon and black light and MUSIC.

DAVE
(handing out shoes)
A few nights later, he asked her out.
He points over to the LANE where they're bowling.

DAVE
They had a good time, and so he asked her again. And then before too long they were seeing each other regularly, and not seeing anyone else.
(MORE)

38.
DAVE (CONT'D)
(THEN)
Of course, Elaine was the only one who knew that...

CUT TO:
EXT. RESTAURANT - PARKING LOT - NIGHT
Roger opens Elaine's door for her, then goes around. She lingers, watches him before she gets in.

ROGER
What.

ELAINE
Nothing...
She smiles; gets in. Roger pauses. CAMERA PANS TO DAVE.

DAVE
Roger has no idea that this was a defining moment for her.
Roger gets in. Fuzzy but not sure why.

CUT TO:
INT. ROGER'S CAR - NIGHT
Roger drives. Elaine looks out ahead. Long stretch of road and no one on it. She turns; looks at him.

ELAINE

Do you realize that, as of tonight, we've been seeing each other for exactly six months?

CAMERA HOLDS on her. She waits.

ELAINE'S INNER VOICE

Gee...I wonder if it bothers him that I said that. Maybe he thinks I'm trying to push him into some kind of obligation that he doesn't want, or isn't sure of. Maybe he's been feeling confined enough by our relationship as it is...

CAMERA PANS TO ROGER.
ROGER'S INNER VOICE

Six months...

39
CAMERA PANS TO ELAINE.
ELAINE'S INNER VOICE

He's worried.

(then thinking about

IT)

Well hey - you know? I'm not so sure I want this kind of a relationship either. Sometimes I wish I had a little more space, so I'd have time to think about whether I really want us to keep going this way. I mean, where are we going?

Are we just going to keep seeing each other at this level of intimacy?

Are we heading toward marriage?

Toward children? Toward a lifetime together? Am I ready for that level of commitment? Do I really even know this person?

CAMERA PANS TO ROGER.
ROGER'S INNER VOICE

So that means it was...let's see...

February when we started going out, which was right after I had the car at the dealer's, which means ... lemme check the odometer...

(he looks down at it)

Whoa! I am way overdue for an oil change here.

CAMERA PANS TO ELAINE. An OVAL IMAGE OF HER APPEARS in the top corner of the screen; they watch him together.

ELAINE'S INNER VOICE
He's upset. I can see it on his face.

ELAINE'S OVAL IMAGE
You know, maybe you're reading this completely wrong - and he wants more from the relationship.

ELAINE'S INNER VOICE
(CONSIDERS IT)
More intimacy...more commitment...

(AND THEN)
-- and maybe what's happening, is he's sensing my reservations?

40
ELAINE'S OVAL IMAGE
Well don't bet the farm on it. But --

ELAINE'S INNER VOICE
-- And that's why he's so reluctant to say anything about his own feelings - he's afraid of being rejected...

CAMERA PANS TO ROGER.
ROGER'S INNER VOICE
And I'm gonna have them look at the transmission again. I don't care what those morons say, it's still not shifting right. And they better not try to blame it on the cold weather this time. What cold weather?
It's eighty-seven degrees out, and this thing is shifting like a goddam garbage truck, and I paid those incompetent lowlife bastards six hundred dollars.

CAMERA PANS TO ELAINE.
ELAINE'S INNER VOICE
-- He's angry. And I don't blame him. I'd be angry too. God, I feel so guilty, putting him through this, but I can't help the way I feel.
I'm just not sure.

ELAINE'S OVAL IMAGE
(TO ELAINE)
You know what your problem is? You're too idealistic. You're waiting for some knight to come riding up on his white horse, when you're sitting next to a perfectly

good person, a person you enjoy being with, a person you truly do care about, a person who seems to truly care about you.

A person who is in pain because of this self-centered, schoolgirl fantasy that you insist on clinging to.

CAMERA PANS TO ROGER. His OVAL IMAGE APPEARS; at the LOCAL BAR with a beer in front of him and pool tables in b.g.

ROGER'S INNER VOICE
They'll probably say it's only a ninety day warranty. That's exactly what they're gonna say, the scumballs.

41
ROGER'S OVAL IMAGE
Let 'em say what they want. You don't have to listen.

ELAINE
Roger?

ROGER'S INNER VOICE
You know you're right. They want a warranty? I'll give them a goddam warranty. I'll take their lousy warranty and stick it right up their --

ELAINE
Roger.

ROGER
(STARTLED)
-- What?

ELAINE
Please don't torture yourself like this. Maybe I should never have...
(BREAKING DOWN)
Oh God, I feel so...

ROGER
(looks over, alarmed)

WHAT --
She struggles to keep control. Her OVAL IMAGE disapproves.

ELAINE

I'm such a fool. I mean I know there's no knight. I really know that. It's silly. There's no knight, and there's no horse.

ROGER

There's no horse?
He looks up; his OVAL IMAGE SHRUGS; gets up off the stool.

ELAINE

You think I'm a fool, don't you?

ROGER

(reacting to the Oval

ROGER)

-- no!
He looks over at her; not sure who he responded to...but it appears he said the right thing anyway.

42.
ELAINE

It's just.. .well I need ...time, I think. I think I need some time.
Roger looks up at his OVAL IMAGE: gone. He looks at Elaine.

ROGER

-- Time. Yes.

ELAINE

(moved, touches his

HAND)

Oh Roger, do you really feel that way?

ROGER

What way?

ELAINE

About time. Do you feel that way about time?
Roger looks confused. His OVAL IMAGE is off playing pool now. He turns to Elaine; does his best to look decisive.

ROGER
Oh. Well. Yes. Yes I do, feel that way. About time.

ELAINE
(MELTS)
Thank you, Roger.

ROGER
-- Thank you.
They smile. Look forward. He looks a little nervous. She looks serene...

CUT TO:
EXT. ELAINE'S APARTMENT BUILDING - NIGHT
Roger drives away. Elaine goes into her building. Already dialing her cell phone...

43.
BLAINE
Come on, Kelly -- pick up.

CUT TO:
INT. ROGER'S APARTMENT - NIGHT
.while Roger and his OVAL IMAGE watch an OBSCURE FOREIGN SOCCER
GAME. Share a giganto bag of Doritos.

ROGER
Hey, Ref - look alive. Those guys were offsides.

ROGER'S OVAL IMAGE
They suck.

ROGER
Who, the Albanians or the Moroccans.

ROGER'S OVAL IMAGE
They both suck.

ROGER
I know.
He eats some more Doritos. But then suddenly-he pauses.

ROGER
I think I missed something back there.

ROGER'S OVAL IMAGE
Wait for the replay.

ROGER
(shakes his head)
No I mean in the car.

ROGER'S OVAL IMAGE
Can't help you. I was shooting pool.
Roger looks up at his Oval Image. It shrugs.

CUT TO:
EXT. A JUICE BAR - DAY
Elaine huddles with Kelly.

KELLY
.and you said 'there's no knight.'

44.
ELAINE
(NODS)
- and no horse.

KELLY
Did you say 'no knight and no horse,' or 'no horse and no knight?'
She looks at Elaine.. This is crucial.

ELAINE
I said 'no knight.' And then I said
'no horse.'

(THEN)
I know he agreed to the knight.

KELLY
But maybe not the horse.

Elaine racks her brain; just can't say for sure.

KELLY
It's probably not important...
(then watching her)
This is really it for you. Isn't it.

ELAINE
(looks at her; nods)
Really it.

KELLY
(glad for her)
Does he know it?
Elaine looks up; she has no idea.

CUT TO:
EXT. LOCAL HOOPS COURT - DAY
Roger and Gene get ready for some 1 on 1. Roger passes to Gene...

ROGER
Check.
.who passes it right back.

GENE
Check.

45.
Roger takes the ball, dribbles, almost starts but doesn't.
Gene looks at him.

ROGER
Listen.

GENE
What.

ROGER
(a beat; then)
-- Elaine and I.

GENE
Elaine and you what.

ROGER
(a beat; then he shrugs)
We sort of have this -- thing.
He looks at Gene. Conveys the full impact of this. Then --

ROGER
Did she ever mention owning a horse?

GENE
Who.

ROGER
Elaine. She ever talk about horses?
Like, to Kelly or something?

GENE
Not that I know of. Why?
Roger thinks.. .then shakes it off. Throws the ball to Gene.

ROGER
What's the score.

GENE
We haven't started yet.
They start to play. CAMERA FINDS DAVE, on a nearby bench.

DAVE
Roger's in love.

CUT TO:
INT. RECORDING STUDIO - DAY
SHERYL CROW takes a break in the MIXING BOOTH.

46.
SHERYL CROW
I can sympathize with your friend, man. I've seen a lot of guys go there.

DAVE
Do you have any advice for a guy in love?

SHERYL CROW
I don't know - most of my songs are about guys out of love.

DAVE
I see.

SHERYL CROW
Cause you know, a guy in love - a guy who's where your friend's at, anyway - they don't know where they are. They're like an ant, standing on a truck tire. They don't know how they got there - all they know is that's not where they were a minute ago. But then they sort of get vaguely okay with it, you know?
They start hangin' out there, they're feelin' pretty good.

(THEN)
Until the thing starts moving.

DAVE
What happens then.

SHERYL CROW
Well then they get crushed.
Dave gulps. She shrugs.

SHERYL CROW
Rock and roll, my friend. Life in the city.

CUT TO:
INT. TWO OLD PEOPLE ON A COUCH - DAY
OLD MAN
November 8, 1960. The day John Kennedy beat Nixon and won the White House. That was the day I met her.
His WIFE turns, looks at him funny.

47
OLD MAN

It was close the whole way - it was neck and neck by God. But then old Kennedy Senior rode on in on that big old pile of money of his, and fixed the results in Illinois. And that made all the difference.

Happiest day of my life, just about.

She watches him. The man is hopeless.

OLD MAN

I was walking away from a newspaper stand, with my head buried in the final edition. And I looked up, and there she was.

(he looks over at his

WIFE)

You were wearing a yellow sun dress and there was a smudge of makeup just over your left eye.

He smiles at her. Gets a thin smile back.

OLD MAN

What.

OLD LADY

That wasn't me.

OLD MAN

Of course it was you. What are you talking about?

OLD LADY

It was your first wife.

OLD MAN

Nonsense.

OLD LADY
(TO CAMERA)

We met in Sacramento. Eight and a half years ago.

OLD MAN

Don't believe her.

OLD LADY

I've never owned a yellow sun dress in my life. And even if I did, I wouldn't be wearing it in November.

48.
OLD MAN
(off her look)
-- The point is, in 1960 an Irish Catholic could be elected president of this fine country, as long as his father was a filthy rich rum-runner with connections to the Mafia! And when Nixon did get elected, he had to quit!
His wife shakes her head.

CUT TO:
INT. KELLY'S LIVING ROOM - DAY
Kelly and Gene on the sofa.

KELLY
Well we didn't know each other. I mean, of course we didn't - we hadn't met yet. But we were both invited to the same party, by different people who we only knew marginally - only the party got cancelled, and I guess that's how marginal we were, because no one told us. So we came in different cars and found ourselves at the same front door - with no one home.
(then taking his hand)
So Gene asked me out to eat.

GENE
I was hungry.

KELLY
You were in love.
(then off his look)
You told me you loved me, that first night!

GENE
I said I loved mashed potatoes.

KELLY
You were eating mashed potatoes.
You said you loved me. You said because your name was Gene and mine was Kelly, that that just proved it.
We were meant to be together.

49.
GENE
(off her look; then

TO CAMERA)
-- Does this have to go in the movie?

CUT TO:
EXT. GENE AND KELLY'S PLACE - DAY
Dave walks out, talks to the CAMERA.

DAVE
Contrary to what many women believe, it's fairly easy to develop a long term, stable, intimate and mutually fulfilling relationship with a guy.
As long as this is the guy:

QUICK SHOT OF A LABRADOR RETRIEVER -- PANTING, FRIENDLY.
DAVE
With human guys, it's extremely difficult. This is because guys don't really grasp what women mean by the term 'relationship.'

CUT TO:
EXT. JERSEY SHORE - DAY
A JERSEY GIRL on break at a SNACK HUT.

JERSEY GIRL
What I don't get is how they can be a fully grown adult male and not be able to make a commitment to a woman who loves him like no one else - and yet the same person, at age seven, could make an unbreakable lifelong commitment to the San Francisco Giants, who do not even know him and who never will.
(shakes her head)
I just don't get it.

CUT TO:
EXT. SEATTLE - E-CAFE - DAY
A SEATTLE GIRL outside the cafe.

50.
SEATTLE GIRL

They're never "ready." If you ask me, guys are in a permanent state of nonreadiness. That's where they live. If guys were turkey breasts, you could put one in a 350 degree oven on the Fourth of July and they still wouldn't be ready in time for Thanksgiving.

CUT TO:
EXT. CHICAGO - RARE BOOKS STORE - DAY
The OWNER arranges titles on a display outside her store.

CHICAGO GIRL
The thing is, you shouldn't even think about marrying them until you really know them. But you can't really know them until you marry them.
(then after a beat)
That's the thing.

CUT TO:
TITLE CARD: "GUY FIDELITY"
EXT. MANHATTAN - DAY
A Manhattan Girl gives a world-weary look.

MANHATTAN GIRL
One: A guy will have sex with anything. Two: A guy will do anything to have sex. There's your Guy Fidelity. Move on.

CUT TO:
TITLE CARD: "GUY PRIDE"
INT. ROGER AND ELAINE'S MARRIED HOUSE - DAY
Elaine and Roger are inside, looking at the front door.

ELAINE
What do you mean, it's 'supposed to be that way.' It's stuck.

51
ROGER
It's basic physics, Elaine. Wood expands. And then, later, it contracts.

ELAINE
But we can't get out.

ROGER

Which also means other people can't get in. That's part of the design - it discourages burglars.

ELAINE
(looks at him)
The same way the toaster was designed to discourage carbohydrate consumption by bursting into flames?

ROGER
That was an outdoor toaster. It was clearly not designed for indoor situations.
The PICTURE FREEZES. DAVE steps in front, talks to CAMERA.

DAVE
I think it's obvious here, that Roger has absolutely no idea what he's talking about. But Guy Pride forces him to keep acting like he does know, for reasons I believe we've covered in an earlier scene.
He nods his head over to the corner, where the CAMERA PANS TO SEE HUDDLED VISIGOTHS, WAITING. Then BACK TO ROGER AND ELAINE as the PICTURE UNFREEZES.

ELAINE
Okay. So now we have a broken water heater and a stuck front door.
(CONTROLS HERSELF;
THEN)
I think it's time to call Steve.
ELAINE'S IMAGE FREEZES. Roger turns to the CAMERA.

52.
ROGER
"Steve."

CUT TO:
EXT. CUL DE SAC - DAY - SLOW MOTION - HEAVENLY MUSIC
STEVE leaves someone's house, heads for his super-outfitted TRUCK. Haloed in golden sunlight. Strong, capable, equipped for every situation.
WOMEN look out from kitchen and bedroom and living room windows, from front steps and yards and gardens, just to see whose house Steve is leaving. The women look all dreamy the way they would in a really corny musical.

DAVE

(watching; to CAMERA)
As far as women are concerned, God didn't really rest on the seventh day. On the seventh day, God created Steve.
As the Women all sigh...

CUT TO:
INT. ROGER AND ELAINE'S HOUSE - DAY
Elaine stands at the basement door. CLANGING down there.

ELAINE
Roger? Did you find anything?

INTERCUT WITH ROGER IN THE BASEMENT
He's in ankle deep water. Pokes a FLASHLIGHT into some of the corners where the overhead bulb doesn't reach.

ROGER
Good news, honey! The basement's level.

ELAINE
How can you tell?

ROGER
Because I know a well built floor when I see one! We were right to buy this house. Everything works just the way it should!

53.
ELAINE
Except there's no hot water.

ROGER
(aiming the flashlight)
Sweetheart, don't you remember? The power company talked about this.

ELAINE
How about calling Steve.

ROGER
(HATES THIS)
We'll call "Steve," when we have a real problem. Okay?

(then more to himself)
A mouse gets the hiccups, you don't have to call Steve every time.

ELAINE
(hears him whang something down there)
But Roger you're such a good copy editor. You don't have to be a good repairman too! Honest!

ROGER
Okay I think I found it.

ELAINE
The problem?

ROGER
The water heater.
Elaine leans her head against the door jam.

CUT TO:
EXT. ROGER AND ELAINE'S HOUSE - DAY
Elaine sits on the step, looking blank. Kelly is with her.
There are LOUD NOISES from the basement.

ELAINE
I don't know why he does this. He doesn't know what he's doing down there...

KELLY
It'll be all right.

54.
ELAINE
(off a loud CLANG)
It's not like some broken part is just going to be standing there, waving a flag that says "Help me."
Or there'll be an octopus on the compressor, and then he could say,
"Look! There's an octopus on the compressor!"

(THEN)
Of course, how would he know it was the compressor...

KELLY

Trust me, it'll all work out. After a while, there's no more harm they can do.

Roger comes around from the side door. SLOSHING feet. Holds a dripping PART.

ROGER

I just need to go to the hardware store. Hi Kelly.

Kelly smiles, waves. Then as Roger sloshes past, to the car.

ELAINE

And what is it about the hardware store? All they do in there is buy a bunch of tools that they don't know how to use -- and no matter what the problem is, all they'll end up doing is whacking at it with a hammer until it breaks even more.

KELLY

And then they cover it all up with duct tape and then come out and say it's supposed to work that way.

ELAINE
(SOLIDARITY NOD)

Then we have to call Steve. And they get offended.

CUT TO:
INT. HARDWARE STORE - DAY

Roger waits at the counter. Talks to CAMERA.

55.
ROGER

Let me tell you something. If I had a dollar for every time I heard "Steve's" name, I could hire somebody better than Steve, just to shake things up. Get her one of these old semi-retired guys - someone from the pre-steroid days, with the hairy shoulders, and the butt crack. They won't be so quick to call him every ten minutes.

The Clerk comes back. Hands over a 53-piece TOOL SET.

CLERK

Remember. Keep these away from anything magnetic.

ROGER
(WINKS)

Got it.

He takes the tool kit from the Clerk and drops it. The Clerk watches Roger chase down all the parts: what a dolt.

CUT TO:
EXT. PARKING LOT - DAY
Roger puts the tool set in his trunk...then stops.

ROGER
The thing is - I missed out.
(turns to CAMERA)
It's like everyone else was there the day they taught all this stuff.
How to look inside acar.Or a furnace. Or a rocketship.But the guys like Steve, youknow.They were born knowing allthis- and now they're laughing.
(MORE)

56.
ROGER (CONT'D)
They all go down to the Competent Guys' Tavern and compare notes.

CUT TO:
EXT. COMPETENT GUYS' TAVERN - DAY
VANS and PICKUP TRUCKS just like Steve's are parked outside.
A STEVE LOOKALIKE gets out and goes in, greeting ANOTHER STEVE also arriving. LAUGHTER pours out from inside.

CUT TO:
EXT. ROGER AND ELAINE'S HOUSE - DAY
Steve rings the bell. Elaine tries opening the door.

ELAINE
(on other side)
I'm sorry - the door's stuck.

STEVE
I can fix that.
He checks it out, taps it in one place and opens the door.
Elaine steps aside, enchanted --
-- as Roger drives up and sees this. And the pain in his heart is something we can feel.

CUT TO:
INT. ROGER AND ELAINE'S BASEMENT - DAY
Power's back on. Steve pulls the cover off the HVAC assembly.
Roger is sorting through the 53-piece tool set he bought and has no idea what to do with.

STEVE
If you've got a minute, sir. I'd like to show you something.

ROGER
(holds up tool kit)
Should I bring these?

STEVE
That won't be --
(then as all the parts

FALL OUT)
-- necessary.

57
ROGER
(LOOKS DOWN)
The latch broke.

STEVE
I can fix that.
Roger puts the tool kit down. Joins Steve.

STEVE
There's your problem right there.

(POINTS)
You got calcification in your pullet- beam header grommets.

ROGER
I was afraid of that.
Steve looks at him. One of those sideways looks.

STEVE

What you gotta do is jack up your laminate bolts and remove the calcification on the stress points.

ROGER
(while Steve takes
SOME MEASUREMENTS)
Of course when he says "you," he doesn't mean "me." I don't have jacks.
I don't have winches. And Steve has got like fifty kinds of each, right on his truck.
If society collapsed, the Steves of the world will be living in nice sturdy shelters that they built with their own hands, eating food that they grew or caught. And I'll be getting shredded to death by wolverines.

STEVE
Here we go.
He reaches down. Pulls out a fuse assembly, holds it up.

58.
STEVE
Here we go. Back in business in no time.

CUT TO:
EXT. ROGER AND ELAINE'S HOUSE - DAY
Steve is packing up his truck. Roger is about to go back

INSIDE WHEN:
KID
Dad, look! Look what Steve made me!
A working battleship made entirely out of Coke cans!
Roger looks. It is a working battleship made from Coke cans.

KID
This is so neat! Thanks, Steve!
The kid runs off. Roger looks at Elaine.

ROGER
Do we have a kid?

ELAINE
Steve got him from the truck.

CUT TO:
INT. STEVE'S TRUCK - TRAVELING - DAY
Dave rides up front with Steve. Talks to CAMERA.

DAVE
Just because Steve can fix things, doesn't mean he's shallow and doesn't have any concerns. All guys have concerns. Deep concerns.

STEVE
(LOOKS OVER)
You like SportsTalk? Mike the Moose?

DAVE
Hell yeah.
Steve gives him a look. Turns on the radio.

59.
CALLER
I'm just sayin' those owners better never run into me. Because God help 'em, man.

MIKE THE MOOSE
-- and we'll pick up on that and more, right after the news.

CALLER
I mean it, man.

CUT TO:
INT. RADIO STATION - WGRG-AM SPORTSTALK - DAY
MIKE THE MOOSE flips a switch; turns to Dave.

MIKE THE MOOSE
Three months ago, the Marlins traded a guy named Rufino Lupenza to the Yankees, for some minor league players and cash. I grant you it was a rotten trade. I grant you the Yankees seem to have this, this knack for making brilliant deals year after year.
But three months?
(pops in a tape)
The Marlins are over it. The Yankees are over it. The players and their families are over it -- but just check this out.

CALLER
(ON TAPE)
The guy was a workhorse! He filled in wherever he was needed and he never got hurt! And when he got hurt, he played hurt.

MIKE THE MOOSE
(ON TAPE)
You know I got a post card from him here at the station. He says they're all doing fine: Lucita's got the kids in their new school already and they all seem happy. She even found an Ecuadorean grocery she likes.

CALLER
Grocery -- the guy batted 340, from both sides.
(MORE)

60.
CALLER (CONT'D)
His on-base percentage was in the
4's, with a rocket arm on defense and an awareness of the field like nobody's business. And they trade him for minor leaguers? For untested, greenhorn punks who can barely even --

MIKE THE MOOSE
(pauses the tape)
That guy's pretty normal.
He cues forward, plays. A GUY CALLER, fighting tears.

MIKE THE MOOSE
(ON RADIO)
You just have to move on, Stan.

CALLER
.I try to - I'm trying. But I just can't make sense of this...
Mike the Moose stops the tape.

MIKE THE MOOSE
These are guys you wouldn't see crying even at a funeral. Guys who can't bring themselves to hug their own children. And they're beside themselves.
(shakes his head)

And all over a meaningless trade...

DAVE
Meaningless?
Mike the Moose looks at him.

CUT TO:
INT. ROGER AND ELAINE'S HOUSE - NIGHT
Roger and Gene are watching the KNICKS/HEAT game. Big bag of Doritos between them.

TV ANNOUNCER
.seventy-seven per cent from the line during the regular season, and a red-hot eighty-three per cent during the playoffs.

ROGER
Stop saying that!

61.
TV ANNOUNCER SIDEKICK
-- and in the fourth quarter of the playoffs, that number is even higher --

GENE
Stop saying that!

TV ANNOUNCER
So they really picked the wrong guy to foul, at this crucial point in such a crucial game.

ROGER AND GENE
Stop saying that!

TV ANNOUNCER
He dribbles. He sets -- he dribbles again...
Roger and Gene lean forward.

ROGER
Come on come on come on comeoncomeon --

GENE

Miss the shot miss the shot miss the shot come on and miss the shot --

TV ANNOUNCER
-- and the Knicks call time out.
They lean back in their seats; breathe some relief.

CUT TO:
INT. KITCHEN - CONTINUOUS
Elaine and Kelly are addressing INVITATIONS by hand. Dave sits on the counter, listens in.

ELAINE
They don't know the players. The players don't know them - yet they idolize these people. They follow them from team to team -- and they know more about these teams than they know about their own families.
They might not even know if they have families.

KELLY
Not during the playoffs anyway.

62.
ELAINE
(amen to that; then)
And what gets me is, they think - they really think - that whether a team wins or loses or not depends on how much they personally care about them. Like if they don't care, the team can't win.

DAVE
But that's true.
They look over - see him on the counter.

ELAINE
What's true.

DAVE
It's true that the level of concern a guy shows for his team can affect the outcome of the game.
(then off their looks)
I mean not just one guy - but lots of guys. All the guys who care about the team combined, if they really care, can make a difference on the scoreboard.

ELAINE
That's crazy.

KELLY
Who is he?

DAVE
(hops off the counter)
-- Follow me.

CUT TO:
INT. THE DEN - CONTINUOUS
Roger and Gene and the game are FROZEN IN PLACE. Dave stands in the doorway with Elaine and Kelly.

DAVE
For the first time ever, through the use of highly advanced technology, we will be able to see the actual Concern Rays emanating from the minds of Roger and Gene, in their attempt to affect the outcome of this upcoming - and totally critical - foul shot.

63.
The PICTURE CHANGES as though a filter has been slipped over the lens. Then we BEGIN TO SEE THE ACTUAL RAYS emanating from Roger's and Gene's foreheads and traveling into the screen. The rays are colored BLUE.

DAVE
These Concern Rays go straight into the television screen where they join the combined Concern Rays of all the other guy fans watching this game right now.

CUT TO:
A MAP OF THE UNITED STATES
Where all the CITIES representing major markets LIGHT UP and FORM ARCS, like airline flight routes, connecting RED or BLUE CONCERN RAYS from each city, and sending them to MIAMI.

DAVE
(in front of map)

Then the rays are transmitted to the actual arena itself, all arriving at the same moment regardless of any geographic or time zone differences.

CUT TO:
EXT. AN ARENA - NIGHT
Dave reports as BLUE AND RED CONCERN RAYS materialize from the sky and descend on the arena, covering the roof.

DAVE
And it is here, at the arena, where the combined Concern Rays from both teams' fans will be measured - not just for quantity, but for quality.
Because this - as every Guy must believe - is what wins ball games.

BACK TO ROGER AND GENE AT THE TV
Dave steps away and the PICTURE UN-FREEZES.

TV ANNOUNCER
He sets...he takes the shot...it's

UP --
ROGER
-- Come on come on come on ---

64.
GENE
Miss the shot miss the shot miss the

SHOT --
ON TV - THE BALL, IN MIDAIR -- BLUE AND RED CONCERN RAYS APPEAR AND CONVERGE ON IT, IN A MIGHTY STRUGGLE FOR DOMINATION TV ANNOUNCER
-- and he misses! He misses! It bounces off the rim and Miami wins the game! What a comeback! A field day for the Heat!
Roger and Gene leap up and scream. High fives, victory dance.
Dave looks at Elaine and Kelly - who look at each other...

ELAINE
Let's get back to those invitations.

KELLY

I'm with you.

They turn, go back to the kitchen. The celebration goes on.

CUT TO:

TITLE CARD: "THE PUBLIC REST ROOM PROBLEM"

INT. MIAMI INTERNATIONAL AIRPORT - DAY

Dave walks down a terminal corridor among hurrying PASSENGERS.

DAVE

If there's one thing women don't know about when it comes to guys, it's the public rest room problem.

And we're here to clear that up right now.

He stops outside a MEN'S REST ROOM, which is currently closed for maintenance.

DAVE

This room is a private hell for a countless number of guys -- yet the women in their lives are completely in the dark about it.

(MORE)

65.

DAVE (CONT'D)

But before we go inside, let's talk with a leading social scientist, so that what we're about to show you sounds a little more official.

CUT TO:

INT. RED CARPET CLUB - DAY

Dave is at the honor bar with the SAME BRITISH GUY. The words "Leading Social Scientist" APPEAR under him this time.

LEADING SOCIAL SCIENTIST

One has to understand that the act of emptying one's bladder goes deep to the very roots of masculinity.

It is an important territorial statement that males are genetically programmed to carry out.

DAVE

I see.

LEADING SOCIAL SCIENTIST

In fact, many of my colleagues believe the reason that dogs howl at the moon is because they can't go up there and urinate on it -- which is not, however, a theory which I embrace. But guess who gets all the grant money every year. The bastards...

He stares off into space. A bitter man.

DAVE
Um...you were saying?

LEADING SOCIAL SCIENTIST
I didn't want this job. Twenty years, in the social sciences? And what was everybody else doing -- they were getting laid. They were going to bed with women. And what have I been doing -- applying for matching grants. And not getting them.
(MORE)

66.
LEADING SOCIAL SCIENTIST (CONT'D)
Applying for any grants at all - and not getting those either. Meanwhile all the "cool dudes" are laughing!

CUT TO:
EXT. "THE COOL DUDES WHO GET THE BIG GRANTS" TAVERN - DAY
Honda Accords fill the lot. TWO MORE drive up and a SCIENTIST gets out of each. They hail each other and go in together.
As they pull open the door, LAUGHTER spills out from inside.

LEADING SOCIAL SCIENTIST (V.0.)
The bastards...

CUT TO:
TITLE CARD: "THE PUBLIC REST ROOM PROBLEM"
EXT. A VIDEO PRODUCTION TRUCK - DAY
There is a SATELLITE DISH on top. Dave is with JOHN MADDEN.

DAVE
With me now is the great John Madden -- legendary coach of football's Oakland Raiders and veteran network analyst for CBS Sports and now the Fox Sports Network. John, thanks for coming by today.

JOHN MADDEN
Happy to be here Dave.

DAVE
John, you heard what our leading expert said about this particular anxiety that guys have regarding bathrooms in general and public ones in particular. Any thoughts?

JOHN MADDEN
Well he's exactly right, Dave. I mean the guy was a little loopy but he hit the nail on the head.

DAVE
So an airport bathroom presents a specific kind of challenge.

67.
JOHN MADDEN
The worst kind, Dave, and in a lotta ways. Because a guy's main goal is to get in and outta there without having to deal in any other way with any other guy - and in an airport bathroom especially, with the turnover rate they've got, he's up against some pretty mean odds.

DAVE
Couldn't agree more, John. Let's go

INSIDE --
CUT TO:
INT. VIDEO TRUCK - DAY - CONTINUOUS
TECHNICIANS wearing headsets. Dave and John sit by a BANK OF MONITORS. There's a TELESTRATOR for John.

JOHN MADDEN
Okay. Now this angle here, we're outside the bathroom and the maintenance guy's just about to open it up.
We SEE THE AREA OUTSIDE THE MEN'S ROOM, WITH "CLOSED FOR MAINTENANCE" SIGNS IN ENGLISH AND SPANISH. A JANITOR starts removing the signs as a BUSINESS TRAVELER heads over.

DAVE
Here's our first candidate now --

INTERCUT WITH:

INT. MEN'S ROOM - CONTINUOUS - ON MONITORS, WITH TELESTRATOR

John diagrams the action, marking up the screen like a football play while the action unfolds.

JOHN MADDEN

Okay now the leadoff guy, he's gonna come in, he's gonna see the open field and he's gonna swing wide right to grab a spot against the wall.

He's got one flank covered this way and for now he's feelin' pretty good -- and of course by doin' that, he's also settin' the tone for everything that happens after. r• . 68.

DAVE

What's the main thing we're looking for, John. What does each individual guy feel he needs to get out of this.

JOHN MADDEN

Well the crucial thing here, is makin' sure there's no eye contact. I mean none - zero. These guys'll look up, they'll look down, they'll look straight ahead -- but a guy would rather have you poke both his eyes out with burning hot fire tongs, Dave, than to give the next guy over a reason to think you might be lookin' at him in a public bathroom. For reasons that oughtta be pretty darn obvious.

DAVE

Obvious indeed. Now here comes Guy Number Two --

The SECOND GUY comes in; John diagrams the call.

JOHN MADDEN

Now Guy Number Two, what he's gonna do is, he's gonna come in, see the first guy in position along the wall and right away he's gonna line up wide on the opposite side. This is a best case scenario here, something both these guys can appreciate.

Plus they've opened up the middle for the third guy --

The THIRD GUY comes in. John diagrams his path to the middle urinal. The Guy goes there.

DAVE

What about eye contact in this situation.

JOHN MADDEN

Well you're still not likely to encounter any, but again if you do, that's what that buffer zone on either side of him's for. And all three of
'em are feelin' pretty lucky to have it, I can tell you that.

DAVE

Okay. Now if things stay like this...

69.

JOHN MADDEN

If things stay like this, you're fine - and if this were some small commuter airport, y'know late at night or somethin', then these guys could possibly even be home free.
But we're talkin' Miami International here, this is the big time, we're talking about 747's, DC-10's, the big jumbo jets dumpin' off three- four hundred people at a clip. So everybody's gonna be next to somebody, which is the last thing any of these guys want. You're in a critical mass situation, and this is where a lotta mistakes get made.

DAVE

Which brings us to Guy Number Four.
Here he comes --

JOHN MADDEN

-- and there he goes...
Guy #4 spins around and leaves. John and Dave watch; then.

DAVE

Now one thing that I know we're going to get asked, John, especially from women, is whether, as guys, we're aware of how utterly stupid this kind of behavior really is.

JOHN MADDEN

Well I think we know, Dave. Don't you think we know?

DAVE

I think we do.

JOHN MADDEN

(NODS)

Have to be stupid not to.

CUT TO:

TITLE CARD: "THE PUBLIC RESTROOM PROBLEM"

70.

DAVE (V.O.)

We did that.

CUT TO:

TITLE CARD: "GUYS AT MIDLIFE"

EXT. UNIVERSITY OF MIAMI - DAY

Dave walks the campus. Threads through GORGEOUS COLLEGE GIRLS who don't know he's there.

DAVE

If there's anything that causes more anguish in a guy than sports anguish, and public restroom anguish, and hardware store anguish, it's the day that he realizes that somehow his life is half over now, and no matter what he tries to tell himself, he's not young anymore and he's never going to be young again.

(then he stops)

And as any guy'll tell you - it sucks.

CUT TO:

INT. AN ELEVATOR - DAY

A GUY IN A SUIT, alone in here. Faint ELEVATOR MUSIC plays.

ELEVATOR GUY

I got used to having the Beatles and Stones called 'classic rock.' Then I heard Elvis Costello on an Oldies station. I figured, okay - who cares - at least it's on somewhere. But then I hear "London Calling," on Muzak. By the Clash. On Muzak.

(SHRUGS)

But what the hell. I'm in a suit and I go around all day explaining peoples' 401K plans to them. And Sting's doing commercials for Jaguar.

He shakes his head; it's hopeless.

CUT TO:

INT. SHOPPING MALL BARBER SHOP - DAY

The BARBER talks while cutting Dave's hair.

71.
BARBER

The way I see it, it's like menopause, right? Except men get it different.

It doesn't show, y'see? The cramps don't come, the hot and cold flashes, and you don't have your magazines and drug stores filled with helpful stuff to do about it. But something comes, and it hits every guy who's living whether he likes it or not. Whether he knows it or not. Guy can lose his bleepin' mind if he doesn't watch out.

He gets a mirror to show Dave the back. Gives him time to get philosophical.

BARBER

But you know? Maybe it's for the better. Maybe whoever designed all this, was afraid to let the men in on what was gonna be happening.

Like if we knew, we'd bail or something. You know, ahead of time.

CUT TO:
INT. A BAR - DAY

The BARTENDER wipes the bar down in front of Dave.

BARTENDER

I'm just telling you what I see.

Every lousy day. A guy'll come in and sit down, right where you are.

He loosens up a little and then it comes. The road not taken.

Unexamined choices. An unfulfilled life. And other guys, they'll come in and don't say a word. The ones who just stare at the mirror.

DAVE

That sounds pretty bleak.

BARTENDER
(SHRUGS; THEN)

I think it goes back to the old times.

Ancient times, you know? When nobody was expected to live past forty.

You got to forty? You died.

(MORE)

72.
BARTENDER (CONT'D)

But now that men aren't doing that, there's a lot more shit up ahead, and none of it looks good so they go freak out and make a mess of things -- they'll quit their jobs or walk out on their marriages or make some other idiot grandstand move. None of them are happy and every single one of them wishes he did something else with his life and can't figure out how it got this way. Every single one of them.

CUT TO:
INT. LAWYER'S OFFICE - DAY
A hotshot LAWYER is dictating a memo to his SECRETARY.

LAWYER
.therefore please be advised that in reference to the aforementioned subject matter, as per the original agreement dated 7 March Two Thousand, --
His Secretary stops writing. Waits.

LAWYER
...7 March Two Thousand...

SECRETARY
Um. You said that already.

LAWYER
(shakes his head)
I started here on the 7th of March.
Fifteen years ago...

SECRETARY
Oh. Well - Happy Anni--

LAWYER
What the hell am I doing. Why did I even think this would be a good idea -- to work my ass off every single day of my life? So I could come in here and dictate letters like this?

SECRETARY
They're not all like this. You do a lot of good...

73
LAWYER

And what does it get me -- a twin- turbo convertible that I don't even get to drive, because I'm always traveling and renting shitbox cars in other cities where all I do is take clients out to lunch and tell them how to negotiate their golden parachutes? You ever sit in the driver's seat of one of those renta cars?

SECRETARY
Well my husband usually does the --

LAWYER
Brand new cars, not even two thousand miles on them, and already they drive like camels. The seat's got no cushion left already, and you're lucky if you don't need a chiropractor after twenty minutes in one. What do people do in those things?

SECRETARY
Maybe I could get you something.
You want something?

LAWYER
Yeah. I want something. I want the number of that hang-gliding place out on Route 33.

SECRETARY
You want to go hang gliding?

LAWYER
I want to teach hang gliding.

SECRETARY
I'm sorry. I didn't know you did that.

LAWYER
I don't do that. I want to do that.
I've always wanted to do that, and lots of other things too -- only I'm stuck doing this all day long. And I don't even know what this is half the time, just that I have to spend every waking hour doing it. So you tell me -- where the hell does hang gliding fit into that.

74.
SECRETARY
Um. Saturdays?

LAWYER
Give me a break.

SECRETARY
(as he starts to leave)
Where are you going?

LAWYER
I should have done this a long time ago.

SECRETARY
What about the letter?

LAWYER
Put in the usual bullshit. Nobody's gonna read it anyway.
He's gone. She sits there.

CUT TO:
EXT. JOHNNY LAKE'S HANG GLIDING CENTER - DAY
JOHNNY LAKE lifts a titanium frame up onto the back of a pickup. Part of it catches on the lift gate and he SWEARS, kicking it. About to really lay into it when the LAWYER drives up in his twin turbo convertible and gets out.

LAWYER
Hi!

JOHNNY LAKE
Sorry. We're closed.

LAWYER
(stunned; watches him)
-- It's two thirty in the afternoon.

JOHNNY LAKE
Hey. I don't make the rules.

LAWYER
Aren't you the owner?

JOHNNY LAKE
You're right. I do make the rules.
We're closed.

75.
LAWYER
(sees he means it)
Look, there has to -- I really want to learn this -- I just quit my job to learn this.

JOHNNY LAKE
Be my guest - learn it.
He kicks the frame again, walks off. The Lawyer watches.

LAWYER
How can you do this? This is the perfect job!

JOHNNY LAKE
Yeah right. Driving around in a rusted worthless pickup truck that's about to be repossessed anyway, while a guy like you, my own age, is going around in a Porsche Carrera.

LAWYER
But you get to fly.

JOHNNY LAKE
No, you get to fly. I get to hoof this shit up and down these godforsaken hilltops listening to stockbrokers brag about getting lap dances from college coeds, and charging the whole thing through the company expense account -- while I can't even deduct my blood pressure medication. That's what I get to do.
He kicks a rock in the road, which almost feels good enough so he kicks another one -- but this one is buried in the dirt like an iceberg and doesn't budge --

JOHNNY LAKE
Ahh, SHIT!
-- and he falls down hobbling on one knee instead.

CUT TO:
INT. ORTHOPEDIC SURGEON'S OFFICE - DAY
Johnny Lake waits on the examining table, holding ice against his leg. The Lawyer sits on the extra chair reading EXOTIC

ISLANDS MAGAZINE.
76.
He holds up a PHOTO: a Guy in a hammock, in Paradise.

LAWYER
Look at this.

JOHNNY LAKE
You got that right.
The Lawyer shakes his head; flips the page.

JOHNNY LAKE
Hey.
(then on Lawyer's look; he shrugs)
You don't think he's gonna...

LAWYER
What.

JOHNNY LAKE
You know. Have to use the --

LAWYER
Glove?
(then off his look)
You hurt your knee. He already took the x-rays.

JOHNNY LAKE
What if something's broken.

LAWYER
Well he's not going in that way.
You don't do a rectal to set a guy's leg.
Still the guy looks doubtful. The ORTHOPEDIC SURGEON -
British, familiar - comes in, with a fresh X-RAY.

ORTHOPEDIC SURGEON
Well you've done quite a number on yourself. Want to see?

JOHNNY LAKE
Why should I. I wouldn't know what the hell I'm looking at. You're the one who went to medical school.

ORTHOPEDIC SURGEON
Don't remind me.
(then on their looks)
What. You think I like this?
(MORE)

77
ORTHOPEDIC SURGEON (CONT'D)
The medical profession? Owing my life to the insurance cartel while the rest of the world thinks I'm so stinking rich?

LAWYER
Well.. .aren't you?

ORTHOPEDIC SURGEON
Of courseIam - I'm an orthopedic surgeon!Ijust don't like people assumingit!

**(THENASHIS BEEPER
GOESOFF)**
And this -- I am so sick of this bloody thing I can't even tell you!
Because every time it goes off it means I have to stop doing one thing I don't want to be doing, and start doing another thing I don't want to be doing. You call that a life?
They look at him. Don't know what to say.

ORTHOPEDIC SURGEON
-- Let me show you something.
(puts down the x-ray, goes to a drawer)
I've been working on this during my free time. Not like I get any.
He gets an accordion-style envelope; takes out a REAM OF TYPED PAGES. Hands it over to Johnny Lake.

JOHNNY LAKE
What is it?

ORTHOPEDIC SURGEON

What is it? It's a screenplay!
This'll blow the lid off the orthopedic surgery industry! Look - look here --
(takes it back; flips

THROUGH)
-- no wait, this part's better. No -- here! Here you go. Read this and tell me if you don't --

78.
He looks up. They're gone.

CUT TO:
EXT. "GUYS WHO WISH THEY HAD DIFFERENT JOBS" TAVERN - DAY
The lot is filled with Ford Fiestas. The Lawyer and Johnny Lake drive up. When they pull the door open there's WHINING from inside...
Then the BARTENDER FROM BEFORE comes out, storms past them and throws his rag down hard as he gets the hell out of there and away from that shit job.
As Dave walks into frame, starts over to his car.

DAVE
Okay! Well it looks like it's time to talk about sex.

CUT TO:
TITLE CARD: "THE PUBLIC RESTROOM PROBLEM"
DAVE (V.0.)
Will you knock it off?

CUT TO:
EXT. SHOPPING MALL PARKING LOT - DAY
Dave gets out of his car and walks towards the mall.

DAVE
For the sake of any younger viewers who might still be paying attention, during this next segment we will be using certain euphemisms to describe a natural and wonderful thing that happens among grownups - grownups besides your parents, that is.

CUT TO:
INT. MALL BOOKSTORE - MAGAZINE AISLE - DAY

Dave walks along all the COSMO'S, REDBOOKS, etc.

DAVE
Probably the fastest growing sector of the U.S. economy is the sector that conducts surveys asking women
(MORE)

DAVE (CONT'D) what is wrong with men. And in all those surveys, there is one main area that shows up constantly at the top of the charts.
(he stops, pulls a

MAGAZINE)
-- Euphemisms.

CUT TO:
INT. VICTORIA'S SECRET - DAY
Dave walks up the aisles filled with delectable things.

DAVE when I say "euphemisms," I of course am not suggesting that guys don't have them. Guys have plenty of euphemisms. Most guys have more euphemisms in a single day - and here I am thinking of a day that occurred in the summer between ninth and tenth grades - than some women have in a lifetime - or longer, in the case of certain Math Teachers.

CUT TO:
EXT. NATURAL HISTORY MUSEUM - DAY
Dave walks outside, past a line of SCHOOLKIDS off a BUS.

DAVE
It all goes back to a time, millions of years ago, when primitive males often had to complete their part of the equation quickly and right away stand ready to fight off attackers.

CUT TO:
INT. NATURAL HISTORY MUSEUM - DAY - CONTINUOUS
Dave walks past glassed-in DISPLAYS of CAVEMAN LIFE.

DAVE
Today, however, women want euphemisms too -- and this ability in males is no longer as prized as it once was.

(MORE)

80.
DAVE (CONT'D)
In fact, when modern women describe the qualities they're looking for in the ideal man, the phrase "a real fast shooter" is usually pretty far down the list.

(THEN STOPPING)
Naturally, it fell to guys to do something about this. So, naturally - they did.

CUT TO:
EXT. A SKI CABIN - NIGHT
Dave stands outside while Kelly and Gene come back from walking their dog. In a hurry.

DAVE one technique for holding back the inevitable, is when the guy - just when he is about to have his euphemism - will hurl himself violently into an iron bed railing, and raise a lump on his head the size of a golf ball.

CUT TO:
INT. THE SKI CABIN - CONTINUOUS
They come in the room, shedding clothes. He lifts her, carries her to the bed -- with nothing but pillows against the wall. He stops, panicked...

GENE
There's nothing there!

CUT TO:
EXT. THE CABIN - CONTINUOUS
Dave watches the LIGHT GO OFF. Turns back to the CAMERA.

DAVE
In cases where there aren't any iron railings, a good backup technique can be found right on the end of the cold wet nose of the trusted family dog.
CAMERA PANS to the window where we hear:

81.
KELLY
Yes...yes...

GENE
.yesyesyesyes...yesyesyesyes...

KELLY
.just hold on...yes...

GENE
.yesyesyesyesYEEE00000WWWW!!!
CAMERA PANS back to Dave.

DAVE
There are also mental techniques --

CUT TO:
INT. ROGER AND ELAINE'S BEDROOM - NIGHT
Roger and Elaine are under the sheets. Some good early MOANING.. .as Dave comes in, holding a mike, interview style.

DAVE
One of the most time honored and reliable mental delaying styles, is the Baseball Method --
(taps Roger's shoulder)
-- how's it going, Champ.
Roger pokes his head out of the blanket; stays active from the neck down.

ROGER
Oh - yeah hi.

(ACKNOWLEDGES CAMERA; then to Dave)
Well, the baseball thing. I mean a while ago I was into that - big time.
You know, fooling around with different lineups, mixing up the batting order - like thinking about what would happen if you took your cleanup guy and made him eighth or something -- just something stupid like that, you know? Stuff you'd never really do.

DAVE
And that did the trick.

82.
ROGER

Oh hell yeah. I mean I could go all night - literally all night - just shuffling my pitching staff around, or thinking about who I might try and sign at the winter meetings.
Hang on --
He goes under the blanket; pays more attention to Elaine... then comes back.

ROGER
The thing is, it got stale. And I found after a while I wasn't enjoying sex or baseball that much. And you don't want to mess with that stuff.

DAVE
(CAN'T DISAGREE)
So what do you do instead?

ROGER
Math problems.

DAVE
Really?
(off his nod)
You mean like if a train leaves Chicago at one o'clock and another train leaves Denver at two o'clock and they're going at different speeds?

ROGER
(shakes his head)
I can't do train ones. I always end up imagining this beautiful girl on the train - and it makes things even worse.
Elaine stops. Pops her head out.

ELAINE what beautiful girl.

ROGER
-- You, Elaine. The girl on the train is always you.

ELAINE
Oh, Roger...

83.
Roger gives Dave a close call look...then goes back to work.

CUT TO:
INT. ROGER AND ELAINE'S KITCHEN - NIGHT
Dave helps himself, makes a sandwich.

DAVE
As you can see, a lot of guys are making a tremendous effort here - and yet, according to certain standards they are still, basically, lame as hell on almost every single count. The reason for this is simple: women set the standards.
(takes a bite)
And not just bedroom standards -- all standards. Because women invented standards. Remember the Dawn of Guys?

CUT TO:
EXT. PREHISTORIC CUL DE SAC - DAY
Long shadows. PRIMATE WOMEN are still at it, pounding roots and dealing with PRIMATE KIDS.

CUT TO:
INT. PRIMATE ROGER AND ELAINE'S CAVE - DAY
Primate Elaine, picking up around the cave. She stumbles on something gross... finally has had it.

PRIMATE ELAINE
(SUBTITLED)
That's it.

CUT TO:
EXT. OUTSIDE THE CAVES - DAY - LATER
Primate Elaine addresses the OTHERS. All SUBTITLES.

PRIMATE ELAINE
I've been thinking. We need some standards around here.

PRIMATE KELLY
What are standards?

84.
PRIMATE BLONDE WOMAN
What is 'thinking?'
The others turn, look at her. Look back at Primate Blaine.

PRIMATE ELAINE
Standards are like rules. Things they'll have to do. And things they'll have to stop doing.

PRIMATE KELLY
How about "no leaving your dirty smelly loincloths wherever you feel like it, and expecting me to do something about it?" Can that be a standard?

PRIMATE ELAINE
That can be one of the first.

PRIMATE BLONDE WOMAN
How about "No gnawing on a fish head during sex?"

PRIMATE ELAINE
There are all kinds of things we can get them to do.

PRIMATE LUCY
How? They're stronger than we are.

PRIMATE KELLY
They smell stronger maybe.

PRIMATE BLONDE WOMAN
(off their laughter)
I like the smell.

PRIMATE LUCY
Of the men, or the rotten fish?

PRIMATE KELLY
There's a difference?
More laughing; then they turn back to Primate Elaine.

PRIMATE KELLY
But how will we make them go along?
Most of them can't even remember which cave to come home to every night. How are they going to remember rules?

85.
PRIMATE ELAINE
We'll give them a Look.

PRIMATE LUCY
A look?

PRIMATE ELAINE
A special look. A 'Certain Look.'

PRIMATE KELLY
But we look at them every day. And they still do whatever they want.

PRIMATE ELAINE
(as the others agree)
I've been working on this. Watch.
She turns to Primate Blonde Woman, who is holding a gourd.
On the Look, the Blonde drops the gourd.

PRIMATE ELAINE
See? And she wasn't even doing anything.
Agreements and "Wows" go all around.

PRIMATE ELAINE
Now who's with me.

CUT TO:
VARIOUS SHOTS, QUICK CUTS OF THE PRIMATE WOMEN TRYING TO GET
THE "LOOK" RIGHT. EVENTUALLY, EVEN PRIMATE BLONDE WOMAN
GETS IT. . .ALTHOUGH AT ONE POINT SHE SCARES HERSELF AND DROPS
THE GOURD AGAIN.
CUT TO:
EXT. TRAIL BACK TO THE CAVES - DUSK
The Primate Guys come back lugging ANIMAL PARTS. Each now has his own ROCK, instead of the giant jagged slabs.

PRIMATE GENE

What are you doing later.

PRIMATE ROGER
I don't know. Probably just stare at the fire.

86.
PRIMATE GENE
A bunch of us are going over to Primate Blonde Woman's cave to see what she does with those gourds.
Want to come?

PRIMATE ROGER
-- Can't. Primate Elaine's ancestors are still here.

PRIMATE GENE
Bummer.

PRIMATE ROGER
Tell me about it.

(THEN)
They are so Ice Age...

CUT TO:
INT. PRIMATE ROGER AND PRIMATE ELAINE'S CAVE - NIGHT
Primate Roger watches Primate Elaine examine his NEW ROCK.
Her PRIMATE MOM AND DAD hover on the edge of the discussion.

PRIMATE ELAINE
I don't get it. What was wrong with the other one.

PRIMATE ROGER
This one's better. It's an upgrade.

PRIMATE ELAINE'S FATHER
What did he say it was called?

PRIMATE ROGER
An 'upgrade.' An improvement on a previous design.

PRIMATE ELAINE'S MOTHER
What? What'd he say?

PRIMATE ELAINE'S FATHER
(to his wife)
An upgrade. An grade.

PRIMATE ROGER
(to Primate Elaine)
The guy said there are newer ones coming out that'll make even this one look primitive. They're getting lighter and rounder every epoch.

87
PRIMATE ELAINE'S FATHER
What guy.

PRIMATE ROGER
Primate Discount Manny.

PRIMATE ELAINE'S FATHER
(MUTTERS)
Boy he must have seen this one coming...

PRIMATE ELAINE
Dad.
(then to Primate Roger)
I just wanted to know what the difference is between this one and the one you had. You were so excited about it when you got it, and now you've gotten rid of it -- and the only difference I can see is where this one has these markings painted on.
She holds it up; something like BASEBALL SEAMS going around.

PRIMATE ROGER
Those make it so it travels better.

PRIMATE ELAINE
Painted on?
(off his look)
-- What'd it cost you.

PRIMATE ROGER

Nothing. A couple wildebeeste steaks and handful of seeds of some kind.

PRIMATE ELAINE'S FATHER
I told you.
(then to his wife)
Did I say he was a bum?

PRIMATE ROGER
Who's a bum. Are you calling me a bum?

PRIMATE ELAINE'S MOTHER
No one's calling anyone a bum.

PRIMATE ELAINE'S FATHER
I'm just visiting. You do what you want.

88.
PRIMATE ROGER
Oh yeah? Who do you think killed your dinner tonight?

PRIMATE ELAINE
Look. Just take it back. Please.

PRIMATE ROGER
But I can't do that! All sales are final!

PRIMATE ELAINE
You can explain it to him. Tell him he can keep the steaks, but we want the seeds back.

PRIMATE ELAINE'S MOTHER
(to Primate Roger)
I don't mean to meddle. But you should listen to your wife.

PRIMATE ELAINE'S FATHER
That's meddling! That's meddling!
(then to Primate Roger)
-- But in this case she's right.

PRIMATE ELAINE

(to her parents)
Look will you both stop?
(then to Primate Roger)
Just take this back. All right?

PRIMATE ROGER
This is totally unreasonable!

(THEN)
Oh I get it. Don't tell me -- it's your time in the moon cycle again --
He stops cold. Stunned by her CERTAIN LOOK. History's first in SLOW MOTION, FROM SEVERAL ANGLES, the way they do it when buildings explode in much bigger movies.

PRIMATE ROGER
-- I'll take it back.
She smiles. FREEZE IMAGE.

CUT TO:
EXT. MIAMI, BAYSIDE COMPLEX - DAY
Dave strolls among the SHOPPERS, TOURISTS etc. He has the ROCK with him; tosses it unconsciously like a baseball.

89.
DAVE
This is basically where we stand today. The only difference is, we have way more standards.
(gives the ROCK to a KID passing by)
There are social standards, about being sensitive - remembering anniversaries, listening during conversations, not eating soup with your hands, or sitting around in your underwear when company's over.

CUT TO:
INT. DEPARTMENT STORE - DAY
Dave goes up the escalator; walks through the kind of 'Home Stylings' section where no other guy would go. Everything he talks about is on display in some form.

DAVE

-- And there are thousands of standards for domestic life, involving even more totally un-guy concepts -- like curtains, bedspreads, napkins, special hangers, little soaps shaped like fruit, and decorative boxes that hold tissues that already come in a box. While guys, left on their own in the wild, will develop lifestyles that don't involve any of these things.

CUT TO:
INT. COLLEGE GUY APARTMENT - DAY
COLLEGE ROGER and COLLEGE GENE stand in their doorway. There is one window, a lot of dust and nothing else.

COLLEGE GENE
I know just what this place needs.

COLLEGE ROGER
(NODS)
Hockey sticks.
They turn around to go buy hockey sticks.

CUT TO:
90.
INT. THE SAME APARTMENT - SOME MONTHS LATER
A RABBIT on a lawn chair drinks beer out of an ashtray.
College Roger and College Gene play Indoor Death Hockey; slamming into walls, scattering NEWSPAPERS and PIZZA BOXES - as their IMAGE FREEZES.

DAVE of course, even by the most basic standards, these two are living like savages. But they honestly don't know this -- because Guys, in their natural state, aren't any more aware of domestic standards than a trout would be aware of the stock market.
And this causes women a lot of concern.

CUT TO:
EXT. SEATTLE - E-CAFE - DAY
SEATTLE GIRL
Take laundry. To him his clean clothes are ready when he's ready to go get them. And they can dry the rest of the way in the drawer. But they don't dry the rest of the way in the drawer, they sit there in damp musty unfolded balls and he doesn't even mind, and I can't figure that out. What is the matter with folding something? What is the matter with waiting for it to be dry?

CUT TO:
INT. DAVE'S CURRENT BEDROOM - DAY
Dave unloads a laundry basket on the bed. Starts folding the clean clothes and making piles.

DAVE
Laundry's a big issue - and a deep and puzzling mystery to guys. My own wife Michelle, for instance, is an accomplished sportswriter and mother of an extremely young child, yet she is still able to maintain a vigorous clothes-cleaning regimen bordering on the super-human. And I'm not allowed near the stuff.

91.
MICHELLE
(comes in with more

CLOTHES)
He's right.
She dumps out the clothes, sees what he's doing and takes over, doing it better. Dave picks up a random BLOUSE, shows a LABEL with lots of printing on it.

DAVE
These are clearly secret codes, that women intuitively understand but cannot adequately explain -- just like how a lot of guys understand the Infield Fly Rule, without being able to explain that.

MICHELLE
I can explain the Infield Fly Rule.

DAVE
Because you're special, Sweetheart.

CUT TO:
TITLE CARD: "GUY BASHING"
EXT. OUTDOOR CAFE - DAY
Dave anchors a semi circle with Sidra, Mia, Karla E and Lila.
They take turns focus group style.

SIDRA

Sometimes I think they're just like tapeworms. You know? I mean tapeworms are just tapeworms - that's all they are, and all they'll ever be. They're just these repulsive little parasitic beasts and nobody expects anything different from them - because people know that's their nature. And it's the same way with guys - although a tapeworm's more likely to help clean out the garage.

LILA
(NODS)
They have to be the biggest and they have to be the best. And they can never back down from a challenge.
Ever.

92
KARLA E
They sleep with your sister and wonder what's wrong with that.

MIA
They will make a game out of anything.
A contest out of anything. Give them a grain of sand and they will figure out some game with it.

LILA
And they'll argue over the rules.

KARLA E
(off their agreement)
They leave their dirty dishes everywhere. I can't believe the places I'll find some crusted over cereal bowl with yuckola blobs of God knows what in them. And the thing is, from his point of view?
They really do get cleaned by magic!
Because I can't take seeing them sit there, so I clean them.

SIDRA
(to Karla E)
I just get him to wash my car when that stuff happens.

KARLA E
Sweetheart he could wash my car with his tongue and it still wouldn't make up for where I find those dishes sometimes.

DAVE
(while they commiserate)
So now that we've heard your thoughts.
The frustration, the exasperation... the obvious question comes to mind:
Why go through it? Why have guys in your life at all?
They look at him.

MIA
-- You mean as a choice? You mean like a mature adult choice to have a guy in your life? In spite of everything?

93
SIDRA
Like trying to borrow money from you, after you've broken up, so he can buy something for his new girlfriend? And wondering what the problem was with that? I mean like really not knowing?
Dave looks at her. They all do. Until --

LILA
I'll tell you why. There is no good reason, that's why.
The others turn, look her way.

LILA
-- I mean don't get me wrong. They really can be fun. You know, like a big stupid dog can be fun. I mean not everything has to be so serious in life. You want to be able to do more with someone than just read book reviews together - which is something a guy would never do anyway.
(then as the others

LISTEN CLOSER)
But what a guy will do? Is at eleven o'clock at night he'll show up at your door and bring cheese steaks.
And he doesn't care that you look all rumply and dreadful from not expecting anyone. He might not even remember that you're a vegetarian and don't eat cheese steaks -- but that doesn't really matter either.
Because the point is he wanted one, and he can't come out and say it but he didn't want to eat it alone.

MIA
And you're the person he thought of.

LILA
(off her look; nods)
I can't tell you what that feels like, when they do that.
(a beat; and then)
I swear, if they knew how adorable they are sometimes, they'd be dangerous. I mean -- more dangerous.
The other Girls think about that. Considering...

94.
SIDRA
-- Bullshit. They're tapeworms.
The rest of them agree and all high-five her. Dave leans back from the fray, turns to the CAMERA.

DAVE
I think it's time for the conclusion now.

CUT TO:
TITLE CARD: "THE CONCLUSION"
EXT. JOHNNY LAKE'S HANG GLIDING CENTER - DAY
A SIGN says "UNDER NEW MANAGEMENT." Dave is on top of the hill, in a rig that the EX-LAWYER is fastening him into.

DAVE
Well now you know where things stand.
You've learned a little bit about guys, and the critical roles they've played in the past and in modern society today. And for better or worse, they're here with us to stay -- so the best thing you can do about it, is continue to learn about them - by coming to see this movie lots and lots of times, and bringing more and more of your friends back every time you do. Because the more people that understand guys, the better for everyone. And the more people that --
(as the Lawyer launches

HIM)
-- WHOAAAAAAAALII
Off he goes. . .right out of frame, and --

FADE TO BLACK.
MUSIC AND END CREDITS BEGIN, AS --

CUT TO:
A PICTURE OF ROGER AND ELAINE, IN ROGER'S CAR
SUBTITLE: Roger now owns a 104-piece tool set, and he has successfully attempted to change his first switchplate.

A PICTURE OF ELAINE WITH HER HEAD AGAINST THE BASEMENT DOOR
95.
SUBTITLE: Elaine has an open line of credit with Steve.

A PICTURE OF GENE AND KELLY, AT A DANCE CLASS
SUBTITLE: Gene and Kelly won the Fred and Ginger Award in three straight ballroom competitions. Gene was right; they belong together.

A PICTURE OF SHERYL CROW, IN CONCERT
SUBTITLE: Sheryl Crow gave a concert in Central Park for half a million people a while back. We weren't there, but we have it on CD.

A PICTURE O
F RICHARD M. NIXON WAVING GOODBYE
SUBTITLE: Richard M. Nixon was finally elected President in
1968. He held that position until August, 1974, when he resigned in disgrace.

A PICTURE OF AGENTS LEOPOLD AND STEARNS
SUBTITLE: Agent Leopold and Agent Stearns were fired by the FBI for gross incompetence. They now work in network television.

A PICTURE OF THE BRITISH GUY WHO PLAYED EVERY EXPERT
SUBTITLE: This man is not really an expert. If you see him, don't listen to any of his opinions.

A PICTURE OF A BALLPLAYER, WITH HIS FACE BLURRED OUT
SUBTITLE: Rufino Lupenza is an imaginary ballplayer, created by the filmmakers to prove a point. However, if he did exist, and if he were any good, the Yankees probably would get him.
And that would suck.

A PICTURE OF JOHN MADDEN ON A TV SCREEN. WHICH THEN COMES
ALIVE --

JOHN MADDEN

Now these are the kinda end credits you like to see. You got the final update thing goin', where you find out how all the characters you've been watchin' are gonna turn out.

You got good music, a lively kinda feel, and maybe most of all, the movie itself isn't too long --

He reacts now, looking down at the TAIL CREDITS as they start speeding up.

96.

JOHN MADDEN

-- that's how you know it's a real movie, in my book. That's how you know it's not some boring kinda art piece made by these tortured head case kids fresh outta film school -- you're not gonna come outta this theater talkin' about symbolism, or the use of darkness and light or any kinda mumbo-jumbo like that -- you come out of this movie and you're laughin'. And that's what I like in a movie - a movie that's funny but it doesn't take forever, you know?

You still got some time to do somethin' after, maybe go get somethin' to eat, y'know? Because the guys behind the thing knew enough not to drag on and on and --

CUT TO:
TITLE CARD: "THE END"
As the MUSIC FADES.. .and it's QUIET. A good quiet...

DAVE (V.0.)
Hey what do you know? We got through the whole entire thing without saying "booger."

FADE OUT:
THE END

Manufactured by Amazon.ca
Acheson, AB

10803020R00055